The
No Bull$#!t
Wine Book

Jonathan Elmore

AuthorHouse™
1663 Liberty Drive
Bloomington, IN 47403
www.authorhouse.com
Phone: 833-262-8899

This book is printed on acid-free paper.

ISBN: 978-1-6655-1129-2 (sc)
ISBN: 978-1-6655-1128-5 (e)

Library of Congress Control Number: 2020925154

Print information available on the last page.

Published by AuthorHouse 12/19/2020

authorHOUSE®

The Introduction

Before we officially begin, I have a confession to make. My name is Jonathan and I am a recovering wine snob. For years, I used fancy words and impossible comparisons to describe wine. Out of a sense of privilege came the snooty behavior. Not to brag, but I've been fortunate enough to have held positions in restaurants, retail, and wholesale that granted me access to all but a few of the best wines in the world. Consequently, my vocabulary began to reflect it. I've also tried some terrible wines and the words I used to voice my opinion about them were equally pretentious in a negative way. I fell into a pattern of trying a new wine and immediately coming up with new and "interesting" ways to describe it. The inane bullshit that would end up in my wine journal was boorish, trite, and unexcitedly academic. It took a fellow salesman to snap me out of the little snob bubble that I had inadvertently built up around myself.

In 2006, I was working for a wine distributor in San Antonio, Texas. As I sat in the sales meeting, we were trying a Chianti Classico that someone had brought in for our team to sample. I smelled it, swirled it, sipped it, swished it, let it sit on my tongue, and swallowed it, letting the lingering esters of the wine settle in my mouth. In my mind, I started to think of how I would write about this wine. "Tart cherry", "slightly singed oak", and "faint heather" were all waiting to be written down in a flurry of praise for this wine. I looked at the guy next to me and said, "That was really good. What do you think of it?" He looked at me and said, "It's good shit and it'll fuck you up."

In that moment, I knew that I had become an insufferable wine snob and I had to change my hoity-toity ways. I had to simplify and eliminate the flowery language so often attributed to wine. Unfortunately, the world needs people to describe wines this way because there are people who demand that type of esoteric trivia. I just knew that I couldn't do it anymore. I had seen the light and heard the message. Like Thoreau said, "Our life is frittered away by detail…simplify, simplify."

In a bold move to redeem my street cred, I started taking words out of my journaling vocabulary. The words are still in my brain, but I reserve them for when there aren't any other words to describe a wine. I relearned how to describe wine so that it sounds like something you would want to buy and actually drink. Even though there are some expert wine drinkers that can find hints of "cedar resin", "leather", "cigar ash", "cat pee", or "bacon grease", those words will not cross my lips again unless I'm describing a saddle or someone's kitty litter box. By the way, those were real descriptive words that I've read and used in the past. Would you buy Chateau de Cat Pee Sauvignon Blanc? I sure as hell wouldn't.

There are always going to be people at both ends of the spectrum when they're critiquing anything. The lofty describe a wine that has "hints of lazy lemon" or "piquant sloe" while others just let you know that this wine is a surefire way to get your drunk on. In this book, I hope to fall somewhere in between. I try to write in a style that most people are comfortable reading. For better or worse, I left all of the curse words in. If you know me at all, you wouldn't believe that I wrote this book unless there were a few sentence enhancers here and there. Keeping that in mind, I hope you enjoy this slightly irreverent look at one of your and my favorite beverages: Wine.

One last thing; like most people who want to let the world in on the fact that they know stuff, I have a website. It started off as a kind of antithesis to the reviews that I was reading. They were flush with internet bravado about how they hated one thing or another and wished the producers would die a slow and painful death. Those people would never say those things if they were face-to-face. But, sitting in their underwear in the consequence-free environment of their grandparents' basement, they said - and continue to say - whatever horrible things they want. The negativity was almost inescapable. There is really only so much of that bullshit you can read without becoming angry and cynical yourself.

So, to counter all of that negativity, I started the "Raves Only" websites The Talking Simian (www. TalkingSimian.com) and The No Bullshit Wine Page (www.NoBSWine.com and it's eponymously named on Instagram). If I try a beer or wine or hear a stand-up comedian that I don't like, I just won't write about it. Why should I waste my energy yakking about something that isn't worth my time? In turn, why would you want to read a long article about something you won't want to try? Writing good reviews about good things is a quicker way to get us all to the good stuff that makes this wonder-filled world a whole lot better.

The *No Bullshit Wine Book* is an extension of that idea. Let's just get to the good stuff and let the peons worry about being negative. If you're ready to get on with it, then we're in agreement.

As a last thought, some people in the wine industry will hate this book. Some will no doubt disagree with what I write about because their experiences were different than mine. I imagine most will probably say it's lowbrow and an oversimplification of such a complex topic. Well, that's kind of the point! I'm here to enjoy myself and share some things you might not know. Hopefully, you'll get some new insights into the wine world. So, without further ado, let's get to the rest of the book.

The Brief and Not Too Boring History Of Wine

As the title of this section might suggest, this is the wham-bam-thank-you-ma'am version of wine history. It's one of those instances when someone else has done a lot of reading and work so you don't have to. I liken it to cheating off your classmate's science homework. You wanted to know about amoebas, but you didn't really want to read the chapter to learn about them. Over many years, I have learned a lot. I have also forgotten a lot, so the dates are vague and the participants are sometimes nameless. However, I have distilled the truly critical information down to the important things, which has made drinking wine a little more fun for me. I would like to share with you what I think are some of the cool parts of wine history.

When I say that I've learned a lot about wine, I mean I have sampled thousands of wines and read far too many books about the subject. Thick books. Books that are so big, they would make you buy an extra seat for one if you brought it on a plane. All of these tomes were heavily laden with facts about the history and origin of each grape species, viticultural area, and wine varietal. They have all of the impossibly intricate information you could ever want to know about wine but didn't know you needed to ask. But they were all missing two things; me and my irreverent sense of humor. Waka- waka!

To be honest, most of those books were boring as shit, and I fell asleep reading them many times. But in my youth, I felt the deep desire to know everything about wine, beer, and spirits. So, I would read and read, thinking that I would develop a posh vernacular that would permit me to rub elbows with the wine snob elite. I didn't know it at the time, but most of the people that I thought were wine intellectuals were really just pretentious assholes that knew as much or less about the topic than I did. The things they were good at were pretending they knew it all and shunning people who made them look foolish by telling them they didn't have their facts straight. As you might imagine from that specific example, that happened to me a few times. It was heartbreaking to be cast aside for being well-read. It was also an important step toward letting go of the idea that wine was a magical elixir that only the top echelon could enjoy. I realized that I was a regular guy that happened to have a healthy love for wine and a good idea of how to talk about it. What I had to learn was how to talk about it in a language we can all understand. All of this has led up to what you have before you, so let's move on to the important part of this History section.

A long time ago in a land far, far away, some guys were growing grapes. They loved eating them but soon discovered that they had too many to eat. One guy said to another guy, "Hey, bro. Let's smash some of these and turn it into juice. That way we can store it before the grapes go bad." Apparently, the other guy thought it was a great idea, so they did just that. What they were unaware of were little things called wild yeast cells. They were, and still are, floating everywhere in the air searching for something to eat. When the wild yeast happened upon these lads' grape juice, it started eating all of the sugars in the juice. The two byproducts of yeast cells eating sugar are carbon dioxide and…wait for it…alcohol! When the two guys went back a couple of weeks later to have some refreshing juice, they slugged down a couple of tankards of free form wine.

From accidents like that, an entire wine culture was created. Truthfully, the far-away land was the Middle East and later, the coastal lands on the Mediterranean Sea. Wild grapes were growing in places like Armenia, Turkey, and Persia from before there were written words. Folklore passed down through generations mentions growing grapes and pressing it for juice. Archeologists have discovered clay jars that contain wine leftovers in Iran and Georgia that date to around 6,000 BC. About that time, the word had gotten around that there was a trick to making wine. Greeks, Italians, and Egyptians were all instrumental in the further development of making wine on purpose instead of it being a happy accident. But they still didn't know what was causing it, they just knew it worked.

From that early development, you can spot wine references throughout literature and historical texts. According to author J. Wilson in his book *"Diary of a Part-Time Monk"*, even the Christian's Holy Bible talks about wine and strong drink 247 times. It has 145 positive references, 62 neutral references, and 40 references about the perils of overindulgence. One of the most famous instances is the wedding at Cana that is written about in the second chapter of John. I'm paraphrasing here but it went down something like this. The wedding reception was hopping and everyone was having fun imbibing. The hosts ran out of wine and they freaked out. Mary asked her son, Jesus, if he could swing a little miracle and solve the problem. Jesus said, "Ain't nothing but a thing, mama" and he turned between 120 and 180 gallons of water into wine. With plenty of wine to be had, the crisis was averted and the party continued with no one the wiser. Besides the Bible, there are plays, novels, and love notes that reference one of the greatest drinks in the world. There are even gods of wine like Bacchus and Dionysus! But until the mid-19th century, no one knew what was turning grape juice into wine.

Enter Louis Pasteur, the father of microbiology (and five kids!). He was commissioned by the French government to figure out why some wines spoiled quickly and some didn't. Through his research and his continuation of experiments started by German scientists, he discovered that little yeast cells were organisms that eat the sugar in the juice. One of the secondary reactions he found was the production of carbon dioxide. This explained why vats of grape juice would suddenly start to bubble and seem to violently boil at times. The other reaction that he discovered was the yeast was converting the sugar into alcohol. Solid in, liquid out. To put it bluntly, the yeast cells were eating sugar which made them pee alcohol and fart carbon dioxide. Try not to giggle the next time you have a glass of wine. The more sugar there was, the longer they ate. The longer they ate, the higher the alcohol content. The higher the alcohol content, the longer the shelf life. Pasteur made great strides in figuring out the process of wine making. As a thank you for finding out this process, France funded some of his non-wine related work. Later, in the 20th century, some folks discovered the exact chemical reactions that happen in wine making. I've read it. It's complicated and super science-y, so I'll spare you the details. Just know that it's pretty cool and in no way should affect which wine you have with dinner tonight. There are literally hundreds of strains of yeast that are used for beer, wine, and spirits production. Each one imparts a different flavor to the end product. Some yeast strains have been kept alive for hundreds of years and used in every vintage. Pretty cool.

One of the coolest things that developed over the years was grafting, or pairing up two different kinds of root stalks to make one. For centuries, most grapes were wild. People could cut a vine or root from their neighbor's grapevine and plant it in their own back yard. Eventually, they would have their own vineyard, but it was still a wild strain of grapes. Some people that were more innovative started to plant two different kinds of wild grapevines in the same hole to see if the best qualities from both grape varieties would make a new super grape. This has become a science unto itself with one of the leading facilities located in Germany, the Geisenheim Grape Breeding Institute in Rheingau. This process of planting two vines together was the birth of grape hybridization. It's how grapes like Cabernet Sauvignon and Pinot Blanc were developed. It was also something that would save the European wine industry from nearly being totally annihilated from a little annoyance called Phylloxera.

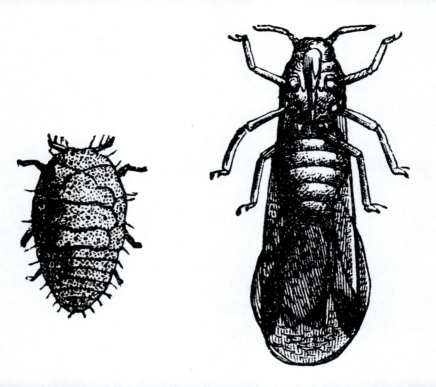

Grape Phylloxera are aphid-like bugs that go by a few different scientific names; Daktu-blah-blah Viti-blah, Phyllo-blah Viti-blah, and insecteous assholeous. These little sap-sucking bastards are native to the northeastern part of the United States. The grapevines that were also native to that area developed a natural resistance to these buggers through evolution or the survival of the adaptable. Through travel and trade, a group of these bugs made their way first to England, then on to mainland Europe. The vinifera grapes that were growing all across Europe had never been exposed to something so vile and destructive. The Phylloxera bugs were like your uncle at a wedding with an open bar. They had free run of the whole continent and they weren't going to stop. In 1875, the total loss of vines was thought to be over two-thirds of Europe's entire vineyard population. As the end of wine production in Europe looked eminent, along came a Texas man to save the day.

Thomas Munson was a botanist, inventor, horticulturalist, and most importantly for us, a viticultualist, or grape scientist. He dedicated part of his extensive career to identifying and cataloging hundreds of different grape species that grew in North America. He then used his knowledge to begin to hybridize them to try to develop new favorable species. Word would eventually reach him that Europe was under siege from Phylloxera. Since part of his research touched on the effects of the bugs on North American plants, he knew that he had a possible solution to Europe's problem. He was going to graft Phylloxera resistant Mustang grape rootstocks to the rootstocks of the European varieties. In theory, the vinifera vines would become at least somewhat resistant to the bugs. Winemakers tensely waited to see if this grafting experiment would work. And it did. The vines that would produce some of the world's best wines were saved by the knowledge of Munson and his colleagues Charles Riley and J. E. Planchon. France was so appreciative that they gave him a prestigious title in the French Legion of Honor. They also made Cognac, France the sister city of Munson's hometown of Denison, Texas. With that, Texas can now say "Remember the Alamo" and "Remember the Phylloxera!"

With the repair and resurgence of European wine production, many countries outside of Europe began looking to them to figure out how they too could grow terrific grapes that made terrific wine. People started to obtain cuttings from thriving vineyards and take them all over the world. Winemakers in France were very forthcoming with their help to populate the world with Cabernet, Malbec, Syrah, Sauvignon Blanc and many other varieties of grapes as long as they got paid, of course. The thought was that if someone can grow a tomato, they can probably grow some grapes. It was a reasonable theory but since no one outside of Europe had attempted to grow any of these grapes, growers in California, Chile, Argentina, and Australia were taking a risk that could pay off big or wipe them out financially. The end of that story is that grapes can grow pretty much anywhere. The middle of the story is a bit more in-depth because grape growers soon found out that not all vines were created equal.

Important for later: A microclimate is an area that has a distinctly different climate than most of the surrounding area. If you're in a fairly desert-like flat area and you find a lush green valley, that valley is a microclimate. Sunlight, shade, soil type, vegetation, water source, proximity to oceans and rivers, proximity to cities, rainfall, snowfall, and cloud cover all contribute to an area's climate. Some microclimates can be quite large, miles wide. Some micros can be as small as the garden in your back yard. In this case, size truly doesn't matter. All the other things listed above are what designates a Microclimate.

Within the climate of the west coast of the U.S., there are dozens if not hundreds of microclimates. One micro in Napa Valley, California can be dramatically different from a micro in St. Helena, California which is only about a fifteen to twenty minute drive to the north. What the pioneers of the wine industry had to figure out was what grapes grew best in what areas. Now, we often take for granted that we have the knowledge that Pinot Noir grapes grow really well in Burgundy, France and Oregon in the U.S. But who figured that out for us? Some of the early planting was done by missionaries from the Catholic Church. They were already out in the world spreading the Gospel and, to properly serve the new parishioners, they needed communion wine. So, past the mission they grew grapes that they had brought from their respective home countries. Most of the time, they did well enough to make the house wine for the Lord. But it would take men and women who studied wine and grapes to figure out what vines would thrive in the unfamiliar fields of Napa Valley, California; Adelaide, Australia; and Mendoza, Argentina.

About the time the U.S. was delving into refined wine production, the government passed the Eighteenth Amendment to the Constitution banning the making, selling, and consumption of all alcohol products. There were a few loopholes for people that were in the alcohol business. Four distilleries were allowed to stay up and running because doctors could prescribe a half pint of whiskey to ailing patients. Some wineries were allowed to make sacramental wine for church services while others turned their fields of grapes into raisins. As a big middle finger in the face of stupid laws, one company offered the Vino Sano Grape Brick. It was a brick-sized block of solid grape concentrate. As a "warning", the package was labeled "After dissolving the brick in a gallon of water, do not place the liquid in a jug away in the cupboard for twenty days, because then it would turn into wine." F. U. Temperance Movement! Eventually, thirteen years later, the ban was lifted with the Twenty-First Amendment. So, our most sacred document now has two entries that make us look like idiots. Luckily, some people went about their daily lives as though the ban didn't matter. The men who ran Catholic missions didn't need to observe a law that didn't apply to them because they were under the protection of the First Amendment. In a small way, this helped to keep the California wine industry in motion while the rest of the country was forced to make terrible bathtub gin.

California had a few guys that came to prominence early on. Brother Timothy from Christian Brothers led the pack. He was a chemist and used this knowledge to produce wines that were much better than those of his 1930's contemporaries. His experimentation and work would also bring Christian Brothers to the forefront of Brandy production in the U.S. Another great contributor is André Tchelistcheff. Don't worry. I can't pronounce it either. He is probably the main guy that brought modern viticulture and winemaking to California. George de Latour started Beaulieu Vineyards (pronounced Bowl-YOU, BV to its friends) and he hired André to head up his winery in the late 1930's. Andre taught George and a few other grape growers about fermentation, barrel aging, and other tricks to get the most out of every grape on the property. Also in the mix were Charles Krug and Robert Mondavi. They were making strides to ensure that California would eventually produce world class wines. Robert Mondavi would become the first winemaker in California to use the actual grape varietal on the label of the wine instead of the vague terms of Chablis, Burgundy, and Rhine. (Some people still use those terms to describe white and red table wines. Stop it. Your terms need an upgrade.)

Mondavi would also be the first to reinvent Sauvignon Blanc. Up to this point, Sauvignon Blanc was blended with whatever other grapes were available and put into jugs. Robert was in France studying wine and he noticed that some wineries were barrel aging their Sauv Blancs. He took that idea back with him to California and even singed the barrels to add a slightly smoky flavor to the wines. The French were calling the wine Blanc Fumé, so just to be different, he called his wine Fumé Blanc. Sneaky! Through a lot of trial and error, these producers discovered which hills should grow Cabernet and which valleys should grow Pinot Noir. It must have been a frustrating endeavor to plant sixty vines on a north coast hillside only to find out that it gets too cold at night for those particular grapes. "Well, dig 'em up and move 'em south! Oops, not that far south." It was the Goldilocks syndrome, too hot, too cold, and just right. I, for one, am very thankful to those early pioneers of the wine industry. Without them, I would have far fewer bottles to choose from at the wine shop.

One final story about California. It's a history making tale, so much so that Hollywood made a movie about it. Bottle Shock was a great movie even though it was more like historical fiction rather than actual events. Basically, the film portrayed Jim Barrett's success as the lucky result of a mistake during Chardonnay production. But in real life, he knew exactly what he was doing. In the early 1970's, Jim Barrett took over wine production at Chateau Montelena. When he arrived, he saw a beautiful piece of property that had been redone by the owners. What didn't meet his standards were the vineyards. Barrett had everything ripped up and replanted. While the older vines were being relocated along with newer vines, he also outfitted the winery with modern winemaking equipment. It was costly but necessary. Since it takes new vines a couple of seasons to produce good fruit, they waited for them to mature and harvested from the older vines.

Finally, in 1972, they had their first harvest of the new plantings. Barrett had successfully figured out which grapes needed to be planted in each acre of the property. That year, the outstanding varietal for them was Chardonnay. It was an off-the-charts kind of tasty. The following year was another stellar vintage of Chardonnay. Barrett had the idea that he wanted to enter their prized wine into an international wine tasting held at the Inter-Continental

Hotel in Paris. The competition was really a chance for French judges to taste French wine and applaud themselves on how much better they were at winemaking than everyone else. In 1973, the judges were to taste four white Burgundies and six California Chardonnays. At the end of the tasting, the judges combined all of their numbers and they had selected what they thought was the best white Burgundy in the bunch. Low and behold, it was Chateau Montelena Chardonnay from the great state of California. The judges were sure they had made a mistake. The Californians were sure that they had officially put their state on the world winemaking map. About the competition, Jim Barrett would later be quoted as saying, "Not too bad for kids from the sticks." Epic.

Similar stories can be related from other non-European countries that have thriving wine industries. Chile and Argentina had to figure out how to deal with growing areas around the Andes Mountains. Through trial and error, Chile has grown to be a top red wine producer rivaling the best Cabernets from France and California. Argentina figured out that they can make good wines, and their Malbecs are possibly the best examples in the world. How did they learn that Malbec was their best chance at world renown? Yep, trial and error. One story that was passed down to me like folklore was the story of the wet rootstalk labels. (I don't know the source, so I apologize for that. If it's you, let me know and I'll give you credit in the next edition.) Some of the French wine masters discovered Argentina had the potential to grow good grapes and hopefully make great wine. They loaded their sailing vessels with hundreds of roots from grapevines that grew all across Europe. As you might imagine, the journey was long and arduous, fraught with sickness and ocean storms.

When they arrived in Argentina, they unloaded all of their rootstalks and winemaking supplies. When they went to separate the grapes, they realized that all of the labels for the roots had been washed clean. There was no way of knowing which root was going to produce which grape. They did the only thing they knew what to do. They just planted everything. Vineyards generally do better when large sections of the same grape are planted together. Those early Argentine vineyards were quite a laughable hodgepodge. The rows were Cabernet – Cabernet – Merlot – Malbec – Sauvignon Blanc – another Cabernet and so on. When the vineyard workers figured out what was what, they replanted them properly. However, since Merlot and Malbec were so similar, they still had the two different vines mixed up. Eventually, the early plantings of the Merlot grapes stopped performing well and the Malbec grapes flourished. Argentina still grows a lot of other varietals. I've had some outstanding Merlots from there, but for that climate and soil, Malbec is king.

Australians were lucky in a way because they waited awhile and learned from everyone else's mistakes. In true Aussie form, they took the casual approach, bided their time, and ended up being a powerhouse in the wine business. They planted vines in all the right places the first time so they didn't have the pain of replanting vast amounts of vines. One interesting fact about Australia is that while the world was busy bottling their wines, Australia was developing the boxed wine industry. In the early years, there wasn't a facility on the entire continent that could make glass bottles. It was far too expensive to ship bottles from Europe or the US, so they put their wines in plastic bladders inside cardboard boxes. The rest of the world followed suit and began putting their inexpensive wines in bag-in-box formats. Wine snobs were revolted. Budget conscious people rejoiced and Australians wondered what all the fuss was about. Eventually, a bottle maker was established in Australia and wineries began using them as well as boxes. Australians were initially distrustful of the bottles, which is a funny turn of thought since the rest of the world was distrustful of boxes. I have more about types of containers and bottle closures in the Other Stuff Section in the back of the book.

The
Wine List

I love a good, organized list, so I decided to make an alphabetical one for all of these different wines. This list does not cover every single wine in the world. Again, I wanted this book to be a manageable size and not overloaded with a bunch of bullshit you'll never see in an average wine store. Don't get me wrong, when you see an oddball wine I didn't write about, go ahead and get it. It will at least be good. It might even be fantastic. Add it to your own list of favorites. But, since most stores stick to the basics, I want to get you familiar with these so you can pronounce and buy with confidence. Always keep in mind that there are expensive and inexpensive versions of most of these wines. The good part is there are tasty versions of both. Don't always let the price tag determine whether it's good or not. Experimentation is the key to expanding your knowledge and love of this great beverage.

I have opted not to include which glassware you should serve these in. Your budget for glassware dictates what glass you serve it in. If you want suggestions, check out the Glassware section in the back of the book.

I have also chosen not to include food pairings with these wines. That either makes me a rebel or lazy. Maybe a bit of both. While it's true that I think Pinot Grigio and shellfish go together quite nicely, you may hate that combination. While I personally wouldn't pair shrimp scampi with Cabernet (and I don't recommend it because strong red wine will overpower any light tasting food you eat making the whole meal unbalanced) you may think that's the cat's pajamas. Knock yourself out. Wine is about what you like, not what other people want you to like. Chardonnay with steak? Do it. Pinot Noir with salmon? Do it. If you're having a meal and you pair it with a wine you don't like, it will ruin the meal. However, do your homework and try what wine experts suggest. You may find it a fantastic combination. If you don't like it, mark it in your wine journal so you don't make that mistake again. If you don't like food pairings that a particular person keeps suggesting, change experts. There are a million suggestions on the internet about what wine to pair with what food. Look them up and make an educated choice. Develop your own list of what tastes good with hamburgers or duck a l'orange. You'll find that certain pairings of food and wine actually do complement each other and the Sommeliers were right all along. Enjoy the list. Cheers!

Amarone (am-a-RO-nay)

This Italian wine is typically a rich, dry red. Amarone translates to "The Great Bitter", which was used to distinguish itself from a sweet wine from the same region. Amarone uses partially dried Corvina grapes to make up the bulk of the blend. This gives the wine a deep purple color and a flavor of black plums and raisins. It has a slightly higher alcohol content than typical red wines, easily above 15%, but it is still very smooth and mellow.

Barbera (bar-BARE-uh)

Barbera is a wonderful Italian wine that has a deep red color, low tannins, and very fruity flavors. The best-known region for this wine is Barbera d' Asti in Piedmont. There are vines in that appellation that have been producing grapes for over a century. Because of the nature of the grapes, these wines are made to drink soon after bottling instead of after a period of cellaring. Wait too long and you'll have ruined your chances of having a great bottle of wine. These younger wines offer hints of cherries and blueberries in both aroma and flavor. Also, if the wine maker wanted wants to add a different subtle flavor, they use charred oak barrels to age the wine, which gives it the faint flavor of vanilla blending with the fruit. I love this wine with pizza.

Beaujolais (BO-szhoh-lay)

This terrific wine is made from the Gamay grape which is thin-skinned and has low tannins. These qualities translate to a smooth, fruity, light-weight wine that is a great match for all kinds of food pairings. It's one of the few reds that you can have with Thanksgiving dinner, and it won't overpower the turkey and dressing. Beaujolais is the main wine from the wine growing region of the same name. There are three tiers to Beaujolais which are Beaujolais (Intro level), Beaujolais Villages (The next step up), and Crus du Beaujolais (Top of the Line). Each tier gets more refined, higher quality, with more dense and complex flavors.

Bordeaux Red (bor-DOH)

Bordeaux has been a wine region since the mid-first century when the expanding Roman Empire planted vines in the fertile soil around the Gironde Estuary. Over time, French laws set up a list of red grapes that are allowed to be grown in the area. They are Cabernet Sauvignon, Cabernet Franc, Merlot, Malbec, and Petit Verdot, and Carménère. These are blended to make some of the best dry red wines in the world. Traditionally, wines from the Left Bank are Cabernet dominant and the Right Bank wines are Merlot dominant. Left and Right simply indicate which side of the Gironde Estuary the vineyard is located. Bordeaux style blends can also be called Claret and Meritage in other parts of the world. For quality control standards, wineries have to pay a fee to be able to call their wines a Meritage, so most don't.

Bordeaux White (bor-DOH)

There are only a few white grape varietals that are allowed by French law to be grown in Bordeaux, : Sauvignon Blanc, Sémillon, and Muscadelle. Most of the dry whites from this area are made from 100% Sauvignon Blanc, while some use small amounts of Sémillon to add a hint of sweetness to the wines. Sweet white wines also hail from Bordeaux. These are made up of any of the three legal grapes that have gone through the process of Noble Rot (See Definition). The most famous of these wines is Sauternes.

Burgundy Red

Also called Bourgogne (bur-GOHN-ya), these dry wines are made up of Pinot Noir grapes. (The exception is the Beaujolais region within Burgundy that grows Gamay grapes to make the Beaujolais wines I mentioned above.) They have a laundry list of different flavors that can be detected in the wine depending on the Terroir (See definition) that they are grown in. They include cherries, strawberries, slate, mushrooms, figs, pears, etc.

Burgundy White

Usually known by its region, Chablis (See Definition), white Burgundies are made mostly from Chardonnay grapes. They are generally dry and affected heavily by the Terroir (See definition) in that area. The land is packed full of limestone, clay, and ancient oyster shells. This imparts light flower and citrus flavors with a hint of minerality similar to mineral water.

Barolo (ba-ROH-loh)

Barolo is a red wine that is made in the northern Italian region of Piedmont. They are made from Nebbiolo grapes and, to some, they are one of Italy's greatest wines. Traditionally, the fermenting juice of the grapes rests with the grape skins for three weeks. That's far longer than most wines. This extracts huge amounts of tannins from the skins and deepens the color. They will then be aged for years before bottling. After that, they sometimes age in bottle for ten years to mature and mellow them to a drinkable level. New producers have begun making the wines to fit a more modern palate by shortening all the above processes, but some claim that they don't represent the true nature of Barolo. I agree.

Brunello di Montalcino (bru-NELL-oh di mont-al-CHEE-noh)

A long time ago, it was believed that there were grapes called Brunello, but thanks to modern DNA testing, they have discovered that Brunello vines are actually Sangiovese vines. The flavors of Brunello were different enough from those in Chianti that they were thought to be a separate varietal. This is proof that Terroir (See Definition) is a true element of wine production. Brunello has become a vineyard designation rather than a separate type of wine made up of 100% Sangiovese. They have flavor characteristics of blackberry, black cherry, black raspberry and chocolate. Don't serve it with any delicate foods. One sip of this wine and you'll never taste your Mahi Mahi.

Cabernet Franc (kab-ur-NAY FRONK)

Cab Franc is planted all over the world and is used mainly for blending with Cabernet Sauvignon and Merlot to add a bit of complexity. When used in blending, it lightens heavier red wines, both in color and taste while maintaining its subtle flavors. By itself, it is generally a lighter style red that has flavors of pepper, raspberry, cassis, and flowers. However, I have seen some dark, intense Cab Francs in my time. In some stores, you might find some bottles of Cab Franc by itself. If you see one, get it. They're wonderful.

Cabernet Sauvignon (kab-ur-NAY saw-vin-YAWN)

At one point in history, Cabernet was the most widely planted varietal in the world. It's now a close second behind Merlot. I don't know who thought that was a good idea, but there it is. Cabernet was everywhere that grapes could be grown. I actually helped take care of a large Cab vineyard in northeast Oklahoma for a little while. In that area, it was sometimes a too hot for too long. We set up temporary canopies that blocked the midday sun and helped the grapes survive the brutal, sometimes week-long 100 degree temperature. When they were processed, the grapes turned into wine quite nicely. I wouldn't put it in a world wine competition hoping for first prize, but it was good table wine.

Cabernet grapes were a happy accident involving the hybridization of Cabernet Franc and Sauvignon Blanc. In France, sometime in the 1700's, the root stalks of those two grapes were grafted together and a hearty, thick-skinned red grape emerged. Those crafty French guys discovered that the left bank of the Gironde Estuary was a primo location for Cab to thrive and produce very high quality grapes. That area of Bordeaux is still considered the pinnacle of Cabernet production. There are other geographical areas that have given Bordeaux reason to sweat the competition. Napa Valley in California has a few microclimates that produce ridiculously tasty Cabs that rival anything the French have to offer. Other sweet spots for Cabernet production are South Australia, Chile, the dry side of Washington state, and a great deal of California. Each viticultural area can endue different taste profiles so it's up to you to search for wines from the different areas so you can find the one you like best. For me, Paso Robles in California is a perineal favorite because the wines don't need to be cellared for years to taste good. They tend to be rich and flavorful without being too dense or too watery. Paso Robles has the baby bear effect, it's just right. (I have not been paid by the Paso Robles wine growers association. I don't even know if one of those exists. If there is, I'm open to bribes and appreciative weekend getaways.)

Like most wine categories, Cabernet Sauvignon varies as you go up the pricing scale. It's not always true, but it's more accurate than not. Lower priced Cabs tend to be simple and fruity like the average Merlot. More expensive Cabs have a tendency to be much more complex and harder to pinpoint all the subtle flavors that are hiding in the wine. There are basic normal flavors like plum, currant, black cherry and mint, but there are also very odd flavors that can be detected like bell pepper, cedar, smoke, and leather. Unless you're a serious wino or a sommelier, the chances of you picking up such traces of the latter list will be rare. Common sense dictates that all you really need to determine is whether you like it or not. The tannins in some Cabernet Sauvignons can be very high and make your face pucker. Aeration usually helps this. Aeration is when you infuse air into the wine. The best way is to decant them by pouring them into a larger vessel like a decanter (best) or a pitcher (budget). You can also fill a glass or two and let it sit out for twenty minutes before you drink it. Both ways will help to calm those tannins down so it won't be so bitter. The reason for higher tannins is that it aids in allowing Cabernet to age for years. There are some Cabs that are decades-old and still taste magnificent. However, most Cabs you find in stores are meant to drink sooner rather than later. If it sits too long, you may end up using it for a nice vinaigrette on your salad.

Carménère (car-min-YAIR)

A member of the Cabernet family of grapes, the name Carménère originates from the French word for crimson which refers to the brilliant crimson color of the vine's leaves before they fall in autumn. Carménère wine has a deep red color and aromas found in red fruits, red berries, and spices. The tannins are softer than those of Cabernet Sauvignon, which makes it a medium-bodied wine. They're perfect to pair with steaks, pork chops, and mushroom dishes.

Catawba (kuh-TAW-buh)

These wines are hard to describe to someone who hasn't tried one. Believed to be a native grape from North America, the grapes are red grapes, but since they are thin-skinned, they don't contribute much to the color of the finished wine. As a result, the wine comes out in varying degrees of pink. The flavors are mild berry, a vague fresh fruitiness, a hint of spice and are usually semi-sweet. You'll find most of these in regional Mom & Pop wineries rather than nationally distributed wineries.

Chablis (shab-LEE)

From the northernmost region in Burgundy comes Chablis wines. They are made up of nearly 100% Chardonnay grapes. Chablis is often confused with cheap low-grade wines from California. When California winemakers were developing, they were using Chardonnay grapes and thought Chablis would be a fitting name for them. The California versions are rare now and usually come in a jug. True Chablis comes from France and is high quality Chardonnay with hints of tart green apple and stony or flinty notes imparted by the limestone soil. Most Chablis is unoaked to highlight the acidity and Terroir (see Definition), but a few choose to age it in oak barrels, which gives it a softer, more complex flavor.

Champagne

All Champagne is sparkling wine, but not all sparkling wine is Champagne. Does that make sense? If it doesn't, it will. True Champagne comes from the Champagne region in Northern France. There are jokes about that like "It's only true existentialism if it comes from the existential region in France. Otherwise it's just sparkling anxiety." Classic.

The naming of sparkling wine is fairly civil. In the E.U., it's illegal to call it Champagne if it isn't from Champagne. In most other parts of the world, they respectfully choose to call it something else. In the U.S., they said, "Fuck you. We do what we want." While most of the wineries in the U.S. respect the title of Champagne and label it by style only, some choose to use the generic term champagne. I usually don't drink those out of respect to France and a solidarity to tradition. That's one aspect of wine snobbery that I'm going to stick to.

Before we get into what makes Champagne and sparkling wine different from still wines, I'll hit you with some of the other names sparkling wines have around the world. This might help you find a cool new sparkler to celebrate with. Some of the names span multiple countries, but know that most are specific to a region that has a similar language like Slavic countries or Iberian countries. Look for Cava and Espumoso from Spain, Sekt from Germany, and Sparkling Wine from the United States and Australia. Italy has Asti, Brachetto, Prosecco, Franciacorta, and Spumante. France has other sparkling wine too. It goes by names like Crémant sparkling wine or simply what the style is; Brut, Extra Dry, etc. Speaking of Brut, Extra Dry, etc., here are the different styles and sweetness levels of Sparkling Wine.

Brut Nature is the driest they come. No added sugar in this one.
Extra Brut is very dry, almost no sugar is added.
Brut is still fairly dry, but it has a few grams of sugar in it.
Extra Dry is a little bit sweeter, but still not noticeably sweet.
Dry, Sec, or Secco is when you really begin to notice the presence of sweetness.
Demi-Sec is like a half sweet/half dry kind of wine.
Doux is super sweet.

Some of the best sparkling wines go through a process called Methode Champenoise (MEH-tod SHAM-pen-waz). Basically, it's a two stage fermentation. The first fermentation is like any other wine; grape juice in a big vat, add yeast, wait, wine. The second part is what differentiates sparkling wine. The wine is transferred into thick glass bottles. The winemaker adds a little bit of sugar and yeast called a dosage (doh-SAHJ) to each bottle. Then, they put a crown cap on it (like a beer bottle cap) and put them in a rack so the bottle is tilted with the cap down. The sugar and yeast go to work making bubbles and giving the wine any special characteristics the winemaker has planned. As the process proceeds, the bottles are riddled. Riddling is when either a person or a machine slightly turns each bottle and tilts it toward the cap so that the excess yeast and sediment slowly fills the neck of the bottle. Once the winemaker is satisfied with the progress, the bottles are cooled, the top of the bottle is frozen, the cap is removed, and the yeast/sediment blob pops out, or is "disgorged" as the professionals like to call it. Before the final cork is installed, they fill the bottle to the proper level and add the amount of sugar they require for the style they want the wine to be.

Next step is the cork, which can be real cork or plastic. Since all the bubbles in the wine are ready to get out of the bottle at any moment, producers use a little wire cage called a Muselet to keep the cork from blowing off the top. Wrap the top in foil, slap a label on it, and it's good to go.

Another method of making sparkling wine, called the Charmat (shar-MAHT) Method, has been adopted by many producers who are making tons and tons of wine. They have altered one of the stages of fermentation so it's a quicker, less costly process. The wine stays in one vat to ferment, then they do the second stage in the same vat. The bubbles still show up, so it's mostly the same. However, most experts can tell the difference. In the Methode Champanoise wines, the flavors are more sophisticated and the bubbles are smaller and more elegant. I know that sounds like a load of hooey, but it's true. Honestly, if you're just making a mimosa or kir royale, subtlety doesn't matter that much. But if you love drinking Champagne by itself, then you should experiment with both styles. You will find, like many others have, that there is a vast difference between a $6 California sparkling whatever and a true Champagne.

Chardonnay (SHAR-doh-nay)

When I started working in a French restaurant in San Antonio, I was a wine newbie. I knew the basics like Cabernet was red and dry, Chardonnay was white and dry, and Riesling was white and kind of sweet. I owe a lot of credit to Frederick, Thierry, and Armand for showing me what good wine is supposed to taste like. Every so often, they would be eating in the dining room and, usually Frederick but sometimes the other two guys, would bring their glass of wine to me at the bar. They would say in their wonderful accents, "Drink this! It is what good Chardonnay is supposed to taste like." I would try it and the taste of it went into my memory. I would thank them and they would usually say, "Oui! Remember this."

From those experiences, I would later try cheap Chards and expensive Chards. I learned that, with everything, there were areas of the world that made better Chardonnay than others. Some of it is subjective, but when a vast majority of wine geeks love a certain viticultural area, it's a safe bet that the area in question is above average. While I don't often drink Chardonnay, I do like a cold glass from a producer in Columbia Valley, Sonoma, or Burgundy. Don't think that those are the only good areas because there are many, many more. I've simply whittled down my preferences and those are my go to areas. Of course, I would never turn my nose up at a glass of wine from other places. That would be rude!

With Chardonnay, the taste profile depends greatly on three things: where the vines are growing, how long the winemaker ferments the juice, and in what vessel the wine is aged.

Where they're growing: The soil and climate contribute a great deal to the outcome of this wine. Some fresh-out-of-wine-school folks think soil and climate have little if anything to do with the end result. Every winemaker that's worth a shit knows better. It matters a lot. Chalky soil and clay soil produce different flavors even if they are in the same viticultural area (AVA). Sonoma County alone has both clay and chalk (and a couple of others) and you can tell the difference if you're paying attention. Dry weather areas and wetter coastal areas produce different flavors. Low temperatures and high temperatures affect the flavor. Imagine trying to be a winemaker now!

How long the winemaker ferments the juice: As a general rule, Chardonnay has subtle flavors of apples, pears, and nuts. The other factors that I mentioned above can add hints of melon, tart green apple, and pineapple. The second thing the winemaker has to consider when they taste the freshly squeezed juice is how long they want the fermentation to last. A short fermentation will give the wine a bright, fruity and refreshing taste. If our wine expert wants something more complex, the wine is put through a second fermentation. Doing this makes the wine naturally develop lactic acid, the same acid that's in milk. This will give Chardonnay the creamy or buttery feel and taste that you may have experienced. These wines tend to be heavier tasting and shouldn't be paired with meals that include cream sauces or heavily buttered dishes. If you're eating butter and drinking buttery wine, you will soon not be able to really taste the food or the wine because your taste buds are coated. As a side note, the lactic acid that develops in these wines does not affect people with lactose intolerance. I read the science behind it and they are different even though the characteristics are similar. Milk? No. Chardonnay? Yes.

In what vessel are the wines aged? There are basically two aging vessels, wood barrels and stainless steel vats. The first method, aging Chardonnay in oak barrels, imparts a hint of vanilla and sometimes a smoky flavor. It also enhances the buttery flavor from the second fermentation. If that's the winemaker's vision, then it is labor intensive and drives up the cost of the wine. It also makes it easy to age Chardonnay for ten years in bottle without any problem. Don't try that with an $8 bottle of Chard. You'll have a lovely vinegar on your hands! The second method is in stainless steel vats. This aging process adds no other flavors to the wine. This keeps the wine crisp, fruity, and uncomplicated. These kinds of Chards go with pretty much any kind of food you want to try it with. There is another method that is a bit sneaky. Some producers reduce costs by aging the wine in giant stainless steel vats and adding planks of oak to the wine. This creates the illusion of barrel aging without actually putting all of that juice into separate casks. It saves room, time, and money. Nothing wrong with that. You get an upgrade on your Chardonnay and it stays at a lower price.

When you're out in the stores hunting for Chardonnay, you may find it under some other names like Macon Village, Pouilly-Fuissé, Bourgogne Blanc, and Chablis. (Although the bulk wines in boxes have the Chablis name and contain some Chardonnay, I'm referring to the real French Chablis.) Happy Chardonnay Hunting!

Châteauneuf du-Pape (SHAT-oh-noof doo POP)

The name for this wine translates to The Pope's New Castle. Every time I see the name, I think of the pontiff sitting in the middle of a giant bouncy castle. HA! I hope you see it now, too. It is a wine from the Rhone Valley in France, and it was originally promoted by Pope Clement V as THE wine to have. This wine is smooth with a silky texture and low tannins. It is usually made up of a blend of Grenache and Syrah grapes, making it a fruity, mellow wine with hints of bright cherry, rich plum and a trace of spice. I actually love this wine so much that I rarely have it with food. But when I do, I choose something you might find in a picture of a French picnic: cheese, baguettes, or a charcuterie extravaganza.

Chenin Blanc / Vouvray / Steen (SHEN-in BLONK)

Chenin Blanc wines have subtle floral and honeydew melon flavors. The aroma from Chenin Blanc can be intensely floral, but it doesn't come through in the taste as much. They are slightly sweet and have a higher acidity level, which makes it a balanced crowd-pleasing wine for parties. All of these characteristics make Chenin Blanc a perfect wine to pair with spicier foods like Thai, Cajun, and Cuban.

Chianti

This wine comes from the DOC region in central Italy. A long time ago, a guy named Baron Bettino Ricasoli came up with the original recipe for Chianti wine. It's 70% Sangiovese (san-jee-oh-VEY-say), 15% Canaiolo (Can-i-O-lo), and 15% Malvasia (Mal-VAY-zee-ah) and that was the law set on the books. Follow that recipe or don't call your swill Chianti. In 1995, the people in charge of Italian wine changed the law so that Chianti could be 100% Sangiovese if the winemaker chose to make it that way. It was a relief to some who preferred that grape over the other two. You may have seen Chianti in a bottle that's half covered in a straw basket. There are only a few wineries that still bottle the wines in *fiasco* (flask) bottles. They're fun to drink while you're having a pizza with friends and some folks reuse the bottles for olive oil, pepper oil, or simply for decoration. There are a few sub-regions of Chianti that you'll see on some wine labels. It's almost like the more words they put on the label, the higher the quality is. Not really, but it could be.

Chianti is wine from the entire region.

Chianti Classico is a smaller area that has is classified as a DOC.

Chianti Classico Reserva is the same as regular Classico except that the wines are made from more select grapes and aged for a longer time.

Chianti Superiore is the cream of the crop within Chianti. It is an even smaller area that has earned the government's approval to be a DOCG. I'll explain more later in the book.

Concord

If you think that this wine probably tastes like grape juice you buy at the grocery store with a little alcohol added in, you would be exactly right. Concord grapes are very sweet, and that sweet juiciness is usually highlighted in wines made from it. They are usually inexpensive, so they make a great introduction to wine drinking.

Dolcetto (dohl-CHET-toh)

This is an Italian varietal grown mainly in the northern part of the country. Dolcetto translates to "little sweet one", but it doesn't necessarily translate to the taste of the wine. Typically, Dolcetto wines are mostly dry red wines that have moderate tannins and wonderful flavors of black cherry, licorice and dried plums. Really good Dolcettos have a perfect balance of dryness, hints of sweetness, and subtle earthiness derived from the area they're grown in. This is a prime example of a wine that not many know about, but definitely should.

Eiswein

It's the same as Ice Wine. I put the info there.

Fumé Blanc (FOO-may BLONK)

Fumé Blanc is Sauvignon Blanc with a twist. Its name was the brainchild of California wine pioneer Robert Mondavi. When Sauvignon Blanc was first being sold in California, it was cheap, kind of sweet, and not very good. Mondavi was in France learning about white wines and discovered the French wineries were making dry, crisp wines from the Sauvignon Blanc grapes. He knew for sure that dry wines would sell in the U.S. so he took all of that new knowledge and brought it back to California with him. After some trial and error, he came up with a fantastic white wine. He flip-flopped the French name Blanc Fumé (another name for Sauvignon Blanc), and it was a success. These days, winemakers who make Fumé Blanc age it in oak barrels for a short time to give the wine a slightly smoky flavor. It still retains the citrus and lemongrass notes, but the barrel aging imparts more complex flavors that pair well with most foods.

Gewürztraminer (guh-VURTS-truh-mee-nur)

If you can't pronounce this wine's name, you can call this wine Gewürz (guh-VURTS). You'll sound hip and cool like you know how to pronounce it, but you don't have time for all of those extra syllables. This wine is a very floral and aromatic white wine. The grapes are red, but winemakers usually strain the skins right away so they don't give any color to the finished wine. Most of the time, it is produced as a semi-sweet to slightly sweet wine on par with German Rieslings. The aroma and flavor both have hints of flowers, peaches, and passion fruit. It pairs really well with spicy Asian cuisine and Cajun food. Oh, I guess it can go with German food too since it came from there! A little schnitzel with Gewürz? Yummo!

Grenache (grehn-AHSH)

This grape is grown everywhere. Well, not everywhere. Everywhere that wine producers have a spare acre, they'll plant a few rows of Grenache. It is used in a lot of red wine blends to soften harsh, heavy wines and make them smoother and less tannic. When it's by itself or the predominant varietal in a wine, it has low tannins, higher alcohol and subtle flavors of strawberry, black cherry and white pepper. Grenache is used extensively in the Rhone region of France where it is revered, as it should be. It can also account for up to 80% of the grapes used in Châteauneuf du-Pape (See Definition).

Ice Wine

Ice Wine, or as our German friends call it, Eiswein, is a style of wine where the grapes are harvested during freezing conditions. The water inside the grapes freezes and, under those conditions, concentrates the sugars and flavors. The grapes are pressed while they are still frozen to draw out a concentrated thick juice. It is then fermented into a thick, sweet wine full of flavors of honey, peaches, figs, apricots, and caramel. Typically, Riesling grapes are used, but winemakers have discovered other grapes like Moscato and Sauvignon Blanc can be used with similar results. They will give the final wine different flavors, but it will still be very sweet. Matching these wines with food can be difficult since they are so sweet. You can add it to the dessert menu with fruit tarts, chocolate mousse, and lemony things. Use it sparingly, and it will make after dinner magnificent.

Lambrusco (lam-BROO-skoh)

There are six basic wine regions in Italy that produce Lambrusco. Like most varietals, it is used for blending, but can also be its own wine with great results. The Lambrusco grapes aren't particularly sweet, so in order to make a sweeter style wine, the winemaker either halts the fermentation before it becomes a dry wine or they add sweeter grapes at the beginning to raise the sugar content. Most Lambrusco wines are semi-sweet to sweet and are often bottled in a frizzante, or fizzy, style. Lambruscos are one of the wines that are a great introductory wine for those novices that want to graduate to an adult beverage, but can't get into the dry style wines just yet. Lambrusco is very food friendly. Drink it with pretty much anything.

Liebfraumilch (LEEB-frow-milsch)

This is a semi-sweet, low alcohol white wine that hails from Germany with the best examples coming from the Mosel valley. The grapes that winemakers have discovered make the best Liebfraumilch are Riesling, Silvaner and Müller-Thurgau. They all have the characteristics to impart a touch of sweet peach to the wine. The low alcohol content and smooth, light, and fruity taste make this a great summer time wine or lunch wine. In Germany, it was often enjoyed with dinner by the whole family, even children. Not that I'm an advocate for young children getting drunk, but a little wine with dinner should be normal instead of feared and despised. As always, be responsible. And don't be a prude. And eat your vegetables.

Madeira (ma-DEER-uh)

Madeira is a Portuguese wine made on the Madeira Islands. Legend has it that the name of the wine came from the name of the islands. (That's me being a smart ass.) The wine is most similar to other fortified wines like Port, Sherry, and Marsala. There are a few styles of it that are made regularly from the four main grapes that grow there: Sercial, Verdelho, Bual, and Malvasia. Like the naming of the Madeira wine after the island, they named each style of wine after the grape it's made from. No point in making things complicated, right? Madeira is a unique wine in that it goes through an aging process called the Cateiro (can-TEE-ro) Method or the Estufagem (es-tu-FAH-jeem) Method. Basically, the difference is the former uses wine casks and the latter uses stainless steel tanks. For both, the wine is heated to accelerate the aging process. This oxidizes the wine which makes Madeira kind of an oddball wine. It's one of the only wines that can be left on a shelf, opened or unopened, for decades and it will still be okay to drink. There have been reports of 200-year-old bottles of Madeira that tasted as good as any wine recently made. That's a good thing if you constantly forget you have wine in the house. Here are the styles of Madeira.

The aperitif style, called **Sercial** (SUR-see-ahl), is very dry and usually has a nutty flavor. Some say it's almonds, but I usually just get mixed nuts and seeds. I suppose that would make it liquid trail mix, but it's tasty. Serve these when everyone is waiting for dinner. It will get their taste buds hyped up for some good food.

The next style is called **Verdelho** (vuhr-DEL-oh). It is a step sweeter than the Sercial. Like all fortified wines, the fermentation process is halted by adding a high alcohol spirit like Brandy to the wine. For Verdelho, they halt fermentation late in the process so it still has a high acidity, and a slight nutty flavor. But with this one, you begin to see the grape's flavors start to show. I would use this one as an aperitif as well. For me, it's a bit too acidic to have with dinner, but there are people who do it all the time because that's what they like. As with every wine I talk about, it's all about what you prefer. Don't let me or anyone else tell you what to like.

One step sweeter is **Bual** or **Boal** (Bohl). This wine has the fermentation halted sooner so that the sugar levels are much more noticeable than the previous styles. This gives the wine a darker color and a medium body (how thick it feels on your tongue). The high natural acidity is eased and the rich flavors of the grapes shine through in a semi-sweet finished product. This wine could be served with dinner, but keep in mind that it has a much higher alcohol content than regular table wine like Cab and Chardonnay. Sip it sparingly or you're going to end up on the floor fighting over a chicken leg with the family dog. And yes, it goes well with chicken whether it's on the floor or not.

The last example of Madeira is called **Malvasia** (mal-VAY-zee-uh) or **Malmsey** (MALM-zee). These are the darkest colored Madeira wines. They have a perfect balance of acidity and sweetness and flavors that lean toward unsweetened cacao, coffee, and caramel (three out of four of my favorite C words). They are sweet but not candy-like sweet which makes them perfect to have with desserts.

There is a fifth grape called **Terrantez** (ter-ROHN-tez) that has had some problems. It almost went extinct, but some responsible adults found some root stalks and are bringing the grapes back to a variety that can be used again to make wine. Hopefully, we'll all get to try some in the near future.

In the face of public demand, The Madeira Islands have planted Tinta Negra grapes to make some of the larger quantities of wine. These grapes can easily be manipulated into the styles that you read about above. They tend to be a lower quality, but taste good. If you see one that is used for cooking or it's pretty inexpensive, it was made with the Tinta Negra. Nothing wrong with that, but it isn't technically a traditional Madeira. I prefer the old school grapes. Maybe I really am still a wine snob. Nah!

Malbec (MAHL-bek)

This red grape is one of the few that was selected to be grown in Bordeaux, France. In blends, it offers body and weight to thinner wines. This helps winemakers save money and still make a decent red blend. By itself, Malbec is a robust red wine with characteristics of blackberries, black cherries, and even earthy fruits like figs and dates. But the important flavors you will find most are the dark berries. The vineyard managers in Argentina discovered that Cabernet and Merlot did pretty well, but Malbec flourished and became more complex than the parent vines that still grow in France. And now, Argentina makes some of the finest Malbec wines the world has to offer. I've had a few of cheap Argentinian Malbecs that are better than some alleged high-end Malbecs from other parts of the world. Experiment with some low-cost Malbecs. You'll see what I'm talking about.

Marsala (mar-SAH-lah)

Marsala wines have a few different expressions. The wine that stays on Sicily, as in not shipped out for export, is usually fermented like regular wines and served like any table wine. But most often, Marsala is a fortified wine like Port, Sherry, and Madeira. Brandy is added halfway during fermentation to maintain higher sugar levels and raise the alcohol content at the same time. There are 8 different classifications of Marsala, but really all you need to know is there are sweet ones and dry ones. While they're nice for drinking as an aperitif or digestive, they can be used in cooking turning okay dishes into interesting dishes. It depends on personal taste whether you use sweet or dry for cooking. While most chefs use the sweet to make things like Chicken Marsala, the dry version is a little more versatile in the kitchen. I personally prefer to use sweet Marsala when I cook that famous chicken dish and then spend the rest of the week drinking the rest of it when I need a little something to take the edge off.

Mead (MEED)

Mead is wine that is made from honey. It is possibly the oldest fermented beverage in history. Although Mead has a strong presence in Norse mythology, the origins of the beverage are lost in time. It's one of those drinks that is so old, no one knows who started making it first. The remnants of it has been found in archeological digs in Africa, most of Europe, and a large part of Asia. Logic would lead us to believe that it was traded by travelers that wandered around all those places. After all, who doesn't want to share something as tasty as Honey Wine?

Mead in its simplest form is just honey, water, and yeast. It can be still or bubbly, sweet or dry, and plain or flavored. Mead can just be honey and water, but it can also contain fruits, spices, berries, grains, and hops depending on what the producer has in mind. Mead's flavor is what you might expect. It tastes like honey. Big surprise! When adjuncts are added (berries, lavender, etc.) it takes on subtle flavors of the things that are added. I've seen some incredibly creative recipes. One in particular was an Earl Grey Tea Mead. The possibilities are fairly limitless.

Another interesting variation for mead is the honey's origin. You can find regional honeys that tastes different from one another because of where the bees get the nectar; sources like clover, dandelions, or even candy. There was a beekeeper who discovered strange colors in the hives at his apiary. He feared that it was a fungus or other contaminate, so he did some investigating. It turned out that there was a candy factory just over a mile from his hives. The bees were dumpster diving in the factory's trash and bringing back a rainbow of colors. Apparently, it didn't affect the taste of the honey, but it looked like a bee circus moved into town.

There are several different styles of mead. There is the regular mead, which is just honey, water, and yeast. A **Metheglin** is a mead that has herbs and/or spices added to it. **Cyser** is mead that is honey, apple juice, and yeast. Exchanging the water for apple juice makes the finished product both sweeter and more tart. A **Melomel** is a mead that has a fruit other than apples and grapes added to it. Apricot and raspberry are popular additions, but any fruit will do. If grapes are added, they're called a **Pyment** for some reason. Who knows? Who cares? A fairly common mixed drink is a Braggot which blends mead and beer. With the various meads and the vast styles of beers, there are more combinations than you can imagine. But it's fun to attempt to try them all like a true Viking.

Mead is quite diverse when pairing it with food. If you have a certain dish in mind, you can probably find a Mead to go with it. From personal experience, it goes well with roast beast, turkey legs, and meat pies. Yeah, I was at a Renaissance Fair. What of it?!

Meritage (MEHR-i-tahzsh)

Meritage is a California invention. In 1988, a few winemakers from Napa and Sonoma started the Meritage Alliance. They wanted to make red and white wine blends like those in Bordeaux but they couldn't legally call them Bordeaux blends. The French are litigiously protective of their wine industry. Not to be deterred, the Californians made up the name Meritage. Now, if a winery wants to have a wine called Meritage, it has to buy its way into the Meritage Alliance or, you guessed it, face a lawsuit. So, smart wineries who don't need to call their wine a "Meritage", simply make a Meritage worthy blend and call it something else. This keeps the cost of their wine down because they don't have the added expense of joining another club. But there are wineries buying in from all over California, and it's spreading to other continents. I'm not saying the name Meritage is completely useless. They do have quality assurances that the wineries must adhere to. Most decent wineries already follow those rules anyway, but the name Meritage assures they do.

Merlot (mer-LOH)

There is a good movie out called Sideways. If you dig this book, chances are you'll like that movie. You may have even seen it already. The reason I bring it up is for one of the epic lines that Paul Giamatti's character says about Merlot. Jack played by Thomas Haden Church says, "If they want to drink Merlot, we're drinking Merlot." Paul as Miles replies, "No, if anyone orders Merlot, I'm leaving. I am NOT drinking any fucking Merlot." Believe it or not, after that movie, sales of Merlot dropped and Pinot Noir sales rose according to Decanter Magazine. It was mostly the under $10 Merlots but it still effected it. This weird, brief moment in wine history was called "The Sideways Effect." Crazy right? What it didn't do was last forever. People that didn't see that movie or forgot about it started drinking Merlot again. Rightly so. It's tasty wine!

Some of the technical information about Merlot is the grapes tend to ripen earlier than most red grapes. Generally, this gives them lower tannins and slightly higher sugar levels than Cabernet. It's nothing really noticeable when you drink it, but science folks have the data to prove it. Grown in the right viticultural area, some higher quality Merlots are usually a dry style similar to

Cabernet and are medium to dark red in color. They tend to exhibit characteristics of currants, blackberries, blueberries, and occasionally mint and chocolate. Lower quality Merlots are usually straight forward fruity wines that are tasty and uncomplicated. What you might imagine when someone says they want a red table wine.

One of the original grapes from the famed Bordeaux vineyards, Merlot is often used as a blending grape to give Cabernet a lighter feel and taste. Some winemakers produce Merlots that are styled like a heavy Cabernet and they can be cellared for up to 25 years with surprisingly delicious results. In Bordeaux, the French discovered that the right bank of the Gironde Estuary was a perfect climate/soil combo for growing Merlot. Truly, some of the most brilliant wines in the world hail from there. And the prices prove that the Bordeaux gangs are proud of their juice. From the vineyards of Bordeaux, Merlot grapes spread all over the world. Unfortunately for us, the taste of Merlot can vary from state to state and continent to continent. It's up to you and me to figure out where our favorites come from. What a terrible thing to have to do; drink more wine! Merlot is one of those wines that can pair with a lot of things, but you should stick to beef, pork, and tomato based dishes like a lot of Mediterranean cuisine. But feel free to drink it while you're sitting in front of your TV watching old Sanford & Son reruns. I know I do.

Montepulciano (MONT-eh-pull-chee-ahnoh)

These grapes are mainly Italian. They grow in tiny patches in other parts of the world, but their main turf is east coast and central Italy. One of the places to find the best Montepulciano wines is in the Abruzzo region. The vineyard managers of the area discovered early that Monty flourished in the area. It grew stout roots and high yields. Usually, when there are more grapes on the vines, the lower the overall quality of each grape. With Monty grapes, that isn't necessarily true. They have the benefit of producing big, fat bunches of tasty grapes that make even tastier wine. The wines made exclusively from Montepulciano grapes are a deep ruby red. They have low tannins and flavors of plums and Bing cherries. The low tannins make it smooth, fruity, and easy to drink. As an added bonus, they are usually fairly inexpensive. Another benefit of the high yield per acre is the availability to sell some of those grapes to producers who are looking to bulk up their own wines. Monty will turn an average tasting blend into something much more palatable. It adds dense color to make red wine blends look more exclusive than they really are. It also adds an interesting flavor profile to the blends. Back to those wines that are made exclusively with Montepulciano grapes. They are not wines that should be kept for great lengths of time. Drink them within five years of its vintage date and you'll be sure to have a great bottle of wine. For food pairing, you can't go wrong with tomato-based Italian cooking. Also, if it seems like a food you would drink red wine with, go ahead and serve it. That's the cool thing about being cheap and easy. Insert your own cheap and easy joke here. Huh-huh. You said, insert.

Moscato/Muscat (mo-SKAH-to / MUS-kat)

Moscato wines are most often rich, thick, and sweet although I've seen a few dry versions. There are both sparkling and still versions of this wine, so finding which style you prefer is a simple matter of trying one of each. A large number of sparkling Moscatos, particularly those produced in Italy, go through a fermentation process similar to Champagne. They are partially fermented in the bottle to add the great bubbles into the wine. For the inexpensive versions, they simply have carbon dioxide injected into it for the same effect. The bubbles aren't as gracefully subtle, but they're in there. Moscato wines are usually lower in alcohol. A general rule is the sweeter the wine, the lower the alcohol. (Not counting fortified wines.)

Being the oldest cultivated grape in the world, Muscat has a couple hundred different varieties that have evolved over the centuries. It is thought that the original Muscat vines were cultivated somewhere around Persia when Persia was Persia and not Iran. From there, the grapes and vines were traded, moved, planted, and cultivated all over the planet. There are even dozens of varieties of Muscat grapes that grow wild all across the U.S. Also, if you've ever eaten a raisin, you have tasted a dried Muscat grape. There's a little fact that will show off your wine nerd skills at parties. The taste profile for most Moscato wines is slightly floral with hints of orange blossom, honey, apricots and pears. If you don't like most wines, but you like these, then there isn't a food that you can't pair with it. The lower alcohol content also means you can drink a little more and not get too sloshed.

Lambrusco (lam-BROO-skoh)

There are six basic wine regions in Italy that produce Lambrusco. Like most varietals, it is used for blending, but can also be its own wine with great results. The Lambrusco grapes aren't particularly sweet, so in order to make a sweeter style wine, the winemaker either halts the fermentation before it becomes a dry wine or they add sweeter grapes at the beginning to raise the sugar content. Most Lambrusco wines are semi-sweet to sweet and are often bottled in a frizzante, or fizzy, style. Lambruscos are one of the wines that are a great introductory wine for those novices that want to graduate to an adult beverage, but can't get into the dry style wines just yet. Lambrusco is very food friendly. Drink it with pretty much anything.

Liebfraumilch (LEEB-frow-milsch)

This is a semi-sweet, low alcohol white wine that hails from Germany with the best examples coming from the Mosel valley. The grapes that winemakers have discovered make the best Liebfraumilch are Riesling, Silvaner and Müller-Thurgau. They all have the characteristics to impart a touch of sweet peach to the wine. The low alcohol content and smooth, light, and fruity taste make this a great summer time wine or lunch wine. In Germany, it was often enjoyed with dinner by the whole family, even children. Not that I'm an advocate for young children getting drunk, but a little wine with dinner should be normal instead of feared and despised. As always, be responsible. And don't be a prude. And eat your vegetables.

Madeira (ma-DEER-uh)

Madeira is a Portuguese wine made on the Madeira Islands. Legend has it that the name of the wine came from the name of the islands. (That's me being a smart ass.) The wine is most similar to other fortified wines like Port, Sherry, and Marsala. There are a few styles of it that are made regularly from the four main grapes that grow there: Sercial, Verdelho, Bual, and Malvasia. Like the naming of the Madeira wine after the island, they named each style of wine

Mourvèdre (moohr-VEH-druh)

One of the grapes that has been grown in Bordeaux for a couple of centuries is Mourvèdre. These outstanding grapes add deep red colors and intense flavors to thinner, paler wines. They bring red Bordeaux wines up to the quality and flavors that they're known for. Outside of Bordeaux, winemakers experimented with varietals that grew around France. Being masterful at their jobs, they created the GSM or Grenache-Syrah-Mourvèdre, a combination of wines that are made in Bordeaux and Burgundy. French law doesn't allow them to be mixed unless they are labeled as Vin de Pays, or just a general product of France. Those winemakers just wanted tasty wine. They didn't care about labels. What happened was Mourvèdre became an interest to other winemakers and has become a viable varietal in wine regions throughout the world. California has a few wineries that offer a 100% Mourvèdre wine and they're all worth sampling. These wines are rich and tannic, higher in alcohol, and have a dense, concentrated fruitiness. If you're pairing this wine with food, you're going to need something that will stand up to the intensity of Mourvèdre. I wouldn't hesitate to have it with a steak, but you can get more creative than that. A Philly cheesesteak, anything you grill or smoke, and tomato heavy foods like Italian can easily match up to Mourvèdre. Try one. Try them all!

Niagara

This is another grape that is native to North America. It is similar to Catawba in flavor and appearance. There are hints of berries, strawberries and spices. They are low in tannins and usually sweet to semi-sweet.

Petite Sirah (peh-TEET si-RAH)

Distantly related to Syrah, Petite Sirah grapes produce a deep purple, robust and slightly peppery wine that really packs in the flavor. Although they are not as popular as Cabernet, Pinot Noir, and Zinfandel, Petite Sirah tends to have the best qualities of all three of those wines. Rich tannins, distinct fruit flavors of plum and currant, and spicy notes make these wines a must have for people who enjoy concentrated, full bodied, dark red wines.

Pinot Blanc (PEE-noh BLONK)

Pinot Blanc is a mutant grape. No, it doesn't have laser eyes or shape shifting abilities. What it does have is a great flavor. It is a mutation of Pinot Noir. Pinot Noir vines which grow red grapes are a little unstable and every once in a while, one of the offshoots will produce white grapes. Those white grapes can be planted and a Pinot Blanc vine is born. These wines have a high acidity which gives them a citrus and floral flavor. Some winemakers age them in oak barrels which softens the acidity and adds hints of vanilla to the finished wine.

Pinot Grigio / Pinot Gris - (PEE-noh GREE-zsheeo / GREE)

There are two basic styles of wine that come from Pinot Grigio grapes. Originally grown in Italy, Pinot Grigio was first produced to be light and fruity with hints of pear and melon. That is the style that is mainly used in Italy and California. The French adopted these grapes and produced Pinot Gris which is a richer, denser version with flavor characteristics of honey, melon and passion fruit. This style is prominent in France and Oregon.

Pinot Noir (PEE-noh NWAHR)

The gap between the high quality and lower quality versions of this wine is broader than that any of the other major wine groups. The flavor of Pinot Noir is chameleon-like in that it can greatly vary depending on the weather, the soil, the seasons, and the direction the hill is facing. I wouldn't be surprise if the wildlife that frequently visits the vineyard doesn't affect this finicky grape. Even Pinot Noirs from the same state in the same county can be very different. These wines can range from simple fruity wines with hints of Bing Cherries and strawberries to complex, rich wines with characteristics of chocolate, figs, violets, prunes, and even fresh mushrooms. Pinots are most often soft, smooth wines with some of the outstanding wines coming from France and Oregon in the U.S.

Port (Sounds just like it's spelled.)

Port is a sweeter fortified wine. The wine is made in exactly the same way as other wines, but halfway through the fermentation, Brandy is added to stop the process by killing the yeast cells that are turning sugars into alcohol. The result is a lot of extra residual sugar in the wine and a significant boost in the alcohol content. Ruby port is a younger usually unaged wine that has a potent, rich grape flavor. Tawny port is an aged wine that loses it's purple color while it sits in the barrels. The caramel colored wine has the flavors of nuts, figs, red grapes, and vanilla. Some ports can easily age for 50 years and come out of the bottle with delicious results. You may see vintage ports out there like 1993 Port or 1972 Port. These are the top-notch Port wines that were harvested in a particular year where both quality and quantity were exactly right. You'll pay a pretty price for them too. Some friends and I pooled our money to try a half bottle of '72. It was amazing! I had to eat peanut butter and jelly sandwiches for a while after paying for it, but it was worth it. Another Port you might see is an LBV, or Late Bottle Vintage. It's basically a port from a single year's harvest and aged four to six years. They usually don't cost as much as a vintage port, but they can be as good as one.

Pouilly-Fuissé (pooh-YEE FWEE-say)

Another name for Chardonnay made in a specific region of France.

Prosecco (proh-SEK-koh)

This is an Italian sparkling wine made from Prosecco or Glera grapes. Same grape, different name. They are usually styled as a Brut or Extra Dry and have a sharp apple flavor with hints of pear, peach and apricot. These wines were never meant to be aged like some Champagnes are. Prosecco should be enjoyed within three years of the vintage date to get the full effect of the fruitiness. As a brunch beverage, it is perfectly suited for Mimosas and Bellinis.

Riesling (REE-sling or REE-zling)

Riesling is a native of Germany where it has been cultivated for hundreds of years. These wines are delicate with flavors of apricots, peaches, honey and subtle spices. They range from dry to very sweet. In most of the world, they are simply labelled Dry Riesling which is what you might think, Riesling which is usually a semi-sweet, and Late Harvest Riesling which is sweet. In Germany, however, the labeling takes on a confusing slant. They are categorized from lowest to highest quality and the list is usually on par with the sweetness levels. I've included all of that information in the Other Stuff section toward the end of the book. Check them out there. The main growing region for grapes in Germany is along the Mosel (sometimes called Moselle) River and the areas you will see the most are Michelsberg and Goldtropfchen. They are both fantastic areas. All you need to do is try a few from both regions to see if you prefer one area over the other. I personally like both equally.

Rosé (ro-ZAY)

These wines are basically lighter style versions of the red wines that they're made from. For a winemaker to produce a Rosé, they leave the grape juice in the tank with the red grape skins for a short period of time. The juice would turn into full red wines if they were left longer on the grape skins, but removing the skins early gives them some of the red and purple hues and imparts hints of the flavors. This gives you a light wine like a white, but with a little more zing. The best versions of these wines are crisp and dry or they have a touch of fruitiness. If you're looking for something to drink with appetizers, salads, and fish, you can easily find a Rosé that you can enjoy with it. Or, y'know, just drink it while you're sitting in the kiddie pool with the dog. No judgement from me. Wines like White Zinfandel and White Merlot can be lumped in with Rosé even though they are a different style of sweet wine. You can read about the difference under the White Zin definition.

Sake (SAH-keh)

Originally a Japanese alcohol beverage, Sake is made from fermented rice. While it is often called a "rice wine" it is actually processed more like a beer than a wine. Depending on the producer, it can be sweet or dry, but they all have hints of flowers, spices, and herbs. Now, there are some producers that are adding flavors like lemon, coconut, apple, and green tea to Sake in order to expand the customers they can cater to. There are two basic types of sake; Futsu-shu and Tokutei Meisho-shu. From there, it gets a little complicated. I'm not afraid to say that it exceeds my knowledge base. Even though I've tried studying it, what I don't know is still greater than what I do know. It's rare that I refer someone to the world wide web, but this is one of those times. I'm still studying Sake, so we can all learn together.

Sangiovese (san-jee-oh-VEY-say)

These are the grapes that are used as the main feature of Chianti and Super Tuscan wines and 100% of the grapes used in Brunello. The wine made from them very often has a bright cherry flavor with hints of strawberry, plum and spices. They are a medium tannin (see definition if you need it) which makes them smooth and fruity while staying a dry wine. Brunello wines, however, tend to be more robust with more concentrated fruit and higher tannins.

Sangria (san-GREE-ya)

When it's pre-bottled, Sangria is a blend of wine and a little bit of fruit juice, a sweetener like honey or sugar, and brandy to raise the alcohol level back to around 10 or 11%. However, a lot of people take pride in their special homemade Sangria recipe. It usually involves a dark red wine like Cabernet or Merlot, chunks of fruit, fruit juice, triple sec, brandy, flavored brandy, honey, sugar, 7up, seltzer, pennies or chewing gum. Well...not the last two, but pretty much anything goes when you're making Sangria at home. There are dozens of recipes out there. You can have fun trying a new one every time you want a refresher.

Sauternes (SOW-turn)

These are French white wines that top the chart on the sweetness scale. They are made from Sauvignon Blanc, Sémillon, and/or Muscadelle grapes. On the vine, the grapes are allowed to go through the process of Noble Rot (see definition). The painstaking process of the production makes these wines fairly expensive to very expensive. The taste of them is heavenly if you like sweet peaches, honey, apricot and hints of almonds. Take one sip of this wine and the flavor will last for a few minutes because of how thick and rich this wine is. If you feel the need to eat something while you enjoy a Sauternes, stick with something like a fruit tart or a lightly sweet pastry.

Sauvignon Blanc (SOV-in-yon BLONK)

Sauv Blanc wines have a noticeable acidity that isn't found in many other wines. They are crisp and tart with prominent citrus flavors, herbs, and sometimes sweet grass. Sauvignon Blanc wines from New Zealand usually have the specific citrus taste of grapefruit while the rest of the world leans more toward a lemon, passion fruit and mandarin flavor. Aging them in oak casks considerably changes the flavor profile to a mellower citrus, rich vanilla, and some have a slight smokiness to them. When that happens, they get their name changed to Fumé. Other names for Sauvignon Blanc are Fumé Blanc, Sancerre, Pouilly-Fumé, Graves, and as a sweet wine in Sauternes.

Sémillon (SEM-ee-yon)

Sémillon is a grape that is used a lot in blending, but it can also stand on its own as a white wine that runs the gamut of sweetness levels. More often than not, it is used to add a touch of sweetness to Sauvignon Blanc and Chardonnay. It's used in nearly every wine producing region so you have probably had some and didn't even know it. But now you do!

Sherry

Sherry is a fortified wine made in and around the Spanish town of Xerez (Jerez). Sherry is a bit of an odd duck when it comes to production. It goes through a fermentation like any other wine, but the process is capped when Brandy is added after fermentation is complete. This results in a dry, higher alcohol wine. The sweetness of some Sherries comes from adding regular table sugar to raise it to the level that the winemaker had in mind. Dry Sherry often tastes very nutty and slightly bitter while sweeter Sherries have a rich caramel and honey flavor. The ranges of Sherry are from Fino and Manzanilla being a light almost table wine style to Oloroso and Amontillado being heavy barrel aged wines to Pedro Ximenez and Moscotel being sweet desert style wines. Cream Sherry is a blend of sweeter style Sherries and is used a lot in cooking. Other good cooking sherries are Golden and Dry depending on the dish that your attempting. It's pretty fun to experiment with Sherries in the kitchen. A little for the food, a little for the chef, a little more for the chef, a little more for the chef…

Shiraz/Syrah (shi-RAHZ & si-RAH)

The two names above are synonyms for the same grape. The only difference is the winemaker's style choice could lead him or her to call it one or the other. In France, they prefer to call it Syrah. The style is generally full bodied and medium to high in tannins so they tend to make your face pucker a little bit. They often have a rich flavor of blackberries, mint, and hints of pepper. Other places that are influenced by the French model of Syrah are Oregon and Washington in the northwestern part of the U.S. and in some counties in California. In Australia, they like theirs to be called Shiraz. They have a tendency to be fruitier and have less tannins and exhibit characteristics of anise, plums and spices. There are also producers in California that have developed similar styles to those of Australia. Like any other wine varietal, your preference depends on you trying a couple of each style to see which one you prefer. And, like any other wine varietal, I like them both.

Steen

This is traditionally what they call Chenin Blanc in South Africa. Since a lot of people wouldn't buy it because they didn't what Steen was, many wineries changed the name to Chenin Blanc to cater to more of the wine world.

Tempranillo (tem-pra-NEE-yo)

This great grape has been grown on the Iberian Peninsula since the time of the Phoenicians. If you don't remember the Phoenicians, don't worry. It's not important in the grand scheme of things. Just know the grapes have been there a long time. Tempranillo grapes ripen earlier than most Spanish grapes. That gained them the name which means "Early". They make robust red wines, but they have a tendency to be somewhat neutral in flavor. This actually makes them good table wines because they…don't NOT go with most foods. I mean, the wines don't have flavors that oppose most foods. Alone they exhibit tastes of plum and strawberry, but it is so subtle that they are usually blended with another grape or two to flesh out a full flavor.

Zinfandel (ZIN-fun-del)

Please don't confuse this wine with White Zinfandel. Although White Zin is made from this grape, it is not a representation of what Zinfandel can be. Zinfandel grapes can produce wines with a wide-ranging variety. Some younger vines produce light, jammy style wines while older vines can produce hearty, robust wines with dark berry and spicy flavors. Red Zinfandel packs plenty of tannins and a slightly higher alcohol content which easily compares to some Cabernet Sauvignons. You may also see terms like Old Vine on some Zin labels. There are four designations for Zin vines and they are as follows:

Old Vine are vines that have been growing for at least 50 years

Heritage Vines are 65 years old

Ancient Vines clock in at 75 years

Historic Vines are 100 Years or older

The reason there is a difference is because as these vines age, the number of grape clusters per acre, a.k.a. the yield, decreases. With fewer grapes on the vines, all the plant's nutrients are going into the grapes that are left. This gives those surviving grapes a richer, more concentrated flavor. You might like it, you might not. The only way to find out is to buy one and try it. Oh no! Another wine tasting! Boo-hoo!

Trebbiano (treb-ee-AH-no)

This is the second most planted grape in the world. The vines produce a lot of grapes, but the wine it yields is often too light in flavor to be used on its own. However, this makes it great as a base wine for more aromatic and flavorful wines. It is also called Ugni Blanc in France and is used solely for the production of Cognac.

Valpolicella (VAL-pohluh-CHELL-uh)

This is a wine region in Italy that is second in production only to Chianti. Its wines are made from a few different grapes that are hard to pronounce, but they are spectacular to drink. They tend to be what a lot of restaurants and families use as an everyday red wine. They are light bodied and very fruity, but deeper flavors are sometime added with the leftover grape skins strained off of Amarone wines.

Vermouth (ver-MOOTH)

Aromatic and herbaceous, these wines are most often associated with Martinis. However, some of the best Vermouth is used as an Aperitif to stir your taste buds before a meal. Every Vermouth recipe is different so it just takes a little trial and error to find the right one for you. Some are simply herbal, but others have hints of orange or grapefruit to give it specific character to use is specialty drinks.

Vinho Verde (VEE-no VEHR-day)

Hailing from the Minho region in Portugal, these are light and refreshing white wines. There can be red, white, and rosé versions, but white is the most common. The literal translation is "Green Wine" but more accurately it is "Young Wine". They usually have a fresh citrus taste with hints of flowers and softer tropical fruit. Vinho Verde wines are often also slightly fizzy. In the beginning, it was because of a second fermentation inside the bottle, but now the second fermentation happens in the winery when carbon dioxide is added.

Viognier (vee-ohn-YAY)

Viognier is very similar to Chardonnay in that it can be a full-bodied white wine. The difference is Viognier is more aromatic and has the taste of apples, pears, and flowers. Some people might scoff at me for this description but it's kind of the halfway point between Chardonnay and Gewürztraminer. And, depending on the winemaker, it can either sway toward one varietal to the other. If you like Chardonnay or Gewürz, give this one a try.

Vouvray/Chenin Blanc (VOO-vray)

Vouvray is the name the French have given to Chenin Blanc wines. It's also called Pineau de la Loire and about twenty other names, but who really has the patience to remember all of that? Just remember that Vouvray is Chenin Blanc and see what it tastes like under the Chenin Blanc definition.

White Zinfandel/White Merlot

These pink wines are different from anything labelled Rosé. They go through what is called an arrested fermentation. It just means that the yeast is taken out long before it turns all of the sugars into alcohol. This causes the juice to be kind of a half wine/half juice blend. They come out very fruity, light and low in alcohol which is why it has become one of the most purchased wines in the world. It can give people who may not like wine a chance to drink an adult beverage. Or they can try some wine without getting into a drier style that they may not enjoy. It's pretty inexpensive too, so it works well if you have a big event where you want to serve wine to a lot of people you don't really know. Finally, why in the hell is it called White Zin if the wine is pink? Back in the 40's, Sutter Home was trying to make a Red Zin. An accident happened and the fermentation process came to a screeching halt. They had a pink, half fermented wine they weren't sure how to handle. The marketing team got to work and came up with the term White Zinfandel as an alternative to Red Zinfandel that was gaining popularity. From a happy accident, as our buddy Bob Ross always used to say, came one of the highest volume wines on the market.

The
Other Stuff

Blends

If you see a wine that has the word Blend on it, like Red Blend or White Blend, it simply means that more that one grape varietal was used in the production. A Red Blend might be made up of Cabernet, Zinfandel, and Malbec. A White Blend might have Chardonnay and Sauvignon Blanc. There are some pretty outstanding wines that are Blends, so don't think they're low class wines or leftover juice. They can be wicked awesome.

Claret (klair-ET)

Claret was originally the name that the British used to identify the wines of Bordeaux. When the Brits started buying the wines, they were very light in style so, using the Latin for "clear", they called them Claret. Now it is a generic term that refers to wines that are in the style of Bordeaux whether they are from France or not.

Crum Rinse

There was an inside joke at Saglimbeni's Fine Wine shop when I worked there. Mike Crum was my wine guru. All the cool shit I learned from that guy is priceless. One thing that he would do when a vendor came to sell us some new wines was called the Crum Rinse. The vendor would pour a small sample of wine. We would taste it and talk about it. Most people might rinse out the glass with water to prepare for the next wine sample. Not Mike. He would have the vendor pour the next wine. He would swish it around the glass and down it like a shot. Voila! The wine glass was now ready for the next wine sample. As a precaution, the Crum Rinse should only be used by professionals. To determine if you qualify, continue reading to the end.

Cuvée (koo-VAY)

When you see cuvée on a wine label, it simply means that it is a blend of a few different grapes or vintages. One of the most prominent uses of the term is in Champagne where the wineries have a tête de cuvée, or a wine that is the top wine that they produce.

Esters

In the wine world, esters are the subtle aromas and flavors that appear in the wines. Depending on the varietal, it can have hints of various flavors like lemongrass, plums, grapefruit, herbs, or minerals without actually having those things in the wine. The climate, terroir, yeast, fermenting vessel and the natural flavors present in the grapes leads to the prominent flavors shining through in the wine. The science of esters is pretty fascinating even though it's very complicated. If it seems interesting to you, by all means, look into it further. If you just want to drink wine and not think about it, you're in the majority. For most wine drinkers, the flavors may be imperceptible. That's perfectly fine. Again, the only thing that really matters is if you like it or not. The one thing I would challenge you to do is read what the winery says about their wine and see if you can find those flavors on your own. If you can, then you've elevated your wine enjoyment. If you can't you're still drinking wine! You're a winner either way.

Here are some Ester words that have been used to describe the flavors of wines. I've used a bunch of these myself, but don't feel pressure to use them unless you can really taste them. Some of these are pretty silly and totally true. They are citrus, berries, and nearly every other fruit in the known universe, lemongrass, honeysuckle and all the flowers you can think of, leather, smoke, tobacco and cigar ash, cat pee, barnyard, wet earth, stones, flint, salt, peppers of all kinds, clove, cinnamon, bread and toast, cream, butter, vanilla, coffee, all the tree nuts, cucumber, mushroom, prosciutto, bacon grease, caramel, vinegar, brown sugar, perfume, black tea, petroleum, Cola, and Chocolate. There are literally dozens more but I'm kind of bored with this list already and I'm sure you are too. Next!

Fermentation

The process to turn grape juice, or any fruit or grain juice, into an alcohol beverage is called fermentation. The grapes are pressed to extract the juice. If it is a red wine, the juice is left to sit with the skins to pull the color out of the skins and into the juice. When the skins are strained out, yeast is added. The yeast eats all of the sugars in the juice. This process converts the sugars into ethanol with a side product of carbon dioxide. When the desired flavors and sweetness levels are reached, the yeast is drained off and the wine is either bottled or aged in barrels. Some wines are fermented a second time in the barrel to produce a different taste profile. Chardonnay is a common example of this process.

Noble Rot

Although it sounds terrible, this is a process to make some of the best sweet wines in the world. There is a gray fuzzy fungus called Botrytis Cinerea that grows on and affects moist bunches of grapes. When the grapes are ripe, the fungus is allowed to grow in the wet conditions, then they are exposed to drier conditions causing the grapes to become raisined. This is what Noble Rot is and they are often said to be Botrytized (BAH-trih-tized). The results is low water content and high sugar content in the grapes. This translates to very rich and sweet wines.

Oenology (sometimes Enology) (ee-NOL-o-jee)

The study of wine. Every aspect of wine knowledge is under the umbrella of Oenology. There are specific fields of study like many other occupations. Law has criminal law, corporate law, entertainment law, etc. Oenology has viticulture, horticulture, microbiology, sommelier, winemaking, etc.

Raisins

Looking across the valleys and hills of California, you will see acre upon acre of vineyards. You might think that's too much wine for one state to produce, but here's what you might not know; a vast majority of those grapes are Muscat grapes and they are used to make raisins. The same wine that makes Moscato wines also makes the tasty sweet raisins you put in your kid's lunchbox.

Sommelier (so-mahl-YAY)

This person is a wine expert that is often employed by fine dining restaurants as a benefit to their guests. A Sommelier can speak with diners and identify what wine would best suit the meal that they are planning to have. And pairing wine with a meal can greatly improve your experience. A Sommelier is required to take a wicked hard test to prove to the International Sommelier Guild that they know their business. They must be able to taste a wine and determine which varietal it is, whether it is new world or old world, what esters are prominent in the wine, what country it is from, what region it is from, and what vineyard it is from. All of that knowledge takes years of training, tasting, and testing. To say that you need a nose for wine to be a Sommelier would be a vast understatement. The grade below Sommelier is Certified Specialist of Wine. They know a lot of the same information as a Sommelier, but it's like the difference between a plumber and an apprentice. A Somm just knows more and they've proven it.

Sulfites

Sulfites can be a pesky little bugaboo for some people. They are compounds that occur naturally in our bodies and in a lot of foods, including our dear friend, Wine. In wine production, extra sulfites are sometimes added as a preservative. If a winemaker doesn't think the wine will sell out in a reasonable amount of time, they might add some more sulfites to extend the shelf life.

Adding sulfites is a pretty common practice since they're almost imperceptible by nearly all wine drinkers. The problem is, even though you can't taste them, they're in there and unfortunately some people are allergic. They can cause maladies like hay fever, wheezing, and hives. Thankfully, there are vineyards and winemakers that have become more natural by eschewing extra sulfites. A few even go so far as filtering the wine to remove some. One way that they are becoming more natural starts in the vineyard.

A lot of vineyards are either organic, biodynamic, or really close to it. It costs extra to become certified organic so they can put it on the wine label. So, wineries simply have organic practices and don't worry about the certification. They often think that the proof is in the bottle, and I agree. Although the term "Organic" is sketchy these days, wineries that claim organic habits are true to their work. They know that if they put out an inferior or harmful product, no one will buy it anymore. These conscientious vineyards don't use chemicals like pesticides and herbicides anywhere near their vines. The vineyard manager passes the unadulterated grapes to the winemaker who doesn't add any sulfites. The result is a cleaner, more natural wine, some of which can be enjoyed by people with mild allergies. The shelf life can suffer a little bit, but more often than not, we're all drinking them in time. Yay for us! If you have an allergy to sulfites, take it seriously. No reason to suffer for wine. There are low sulfite wines to enjoy even if you have to special order them from your local wine shop.

Tannins

Tannins are in a lot of things like coffee, berries, basil, and rosemary. But, since this is a wine book, we'll stick to the topic at hand. Tannins are basically the naturally occurring compounds in grapes and red wine that make your face pucker. All grapes have different levels of tannins in their skins. Depending on the winemaker's vision, a wine can have trace amounts or super heavy amounts. Even wines within the same category, like Cabernet for instance, can range from soft, easy tannins to deep, robust tannins. The only way to find your preference is to drink more. Oh, the agony!

Terroir (tehr-WAHR)

This term can be confusing when wine snobs throw it around assuming you know what they're talking about. What it means is the total natural environment in which a particular wine is produced. This includes factors such as what type of soil the vines are in, topography or lay of the land, and climate like rainfall, temperature and foggy conditions. Some experts question the true impact of Terroir on the final outcome of wine, but centuries of planting grafts of the same plant on different continents lends itself as proof that the same vines can be affected by where they're grown. Grapes from the same state, county, and Viticultural Area can have different flavors because one set of vines is planted in clay and the other is planted in limestone. It may not be noticeable or important to the average wine drinker, but some folks can tell and it can make a difference to us.

Viticulture and Viniculture

These two are very similar in that they both deal with grapevine agriculture. A Viticulturist practices the science and production of all grapes. A Viniculturist deals specifically with grapes used for winemaking. They can be interchangeable in certain situations, but someone who is a specialist in Thompson grapes that you buy at the grocery store may not be able to determine if Pinot Noir grapes are ready to harvest. It's like specialized doctors. You wouldn't go see an oncologist for a hernia surgery. They're both educated, just in different areas.

Viticultural Area

In the U.S., there are AVAs or American Viticultural Areas. As I write this, there are 214 AVAs and more on the way. Some you may have seen before are Napa Valley, Sonoma County, Finger Lakes, and Texas Hill Country. In the rest of the world, the term Appellation is used to indicate specific regions that grapes are grown. In Italy, a couple are Tuscany and Piedmont. France has Bordeaux and Burgundy. All of them have subregions that are their own designation, but that's a lot of extra information to cover here.

Wine 101: Storing and Pouring

Closures: Cork, Cap, Box and Beyond

Now, there are some very delicious wines that I've started calling Cardboardeaux. There is a little experiment you can try at your next party that will prove a point to everyone. It's a fun trick to put boxed wine in a decanter and set it out at a party. People will ask what it is and you have to wait until the end of the party to reveal that it was Bota Box Old Vine Zinfandel the whole time. They'll be humbled to know that a tasty wine didn't come from a bottle that had a real cork in it. This leads me to the last section of wine history; the cork.

For ages, wine and distilled spirits were bottled and corks were used to keep all the liquid goodness inside. Traditional corks are an organic product, not in the modern sense of "Certified Organic", but it comes from a living thing. Cork is tree bark from the aptly named Cork Oak tree that grows in regions of Europe and northern Africa, with a larger percentage coming from Spain and Portugal. It's a sustainable crop since the trees regenerate the bark that is harvested. Obviously, natural cork can be shaped and used as bottle stoppers. They can also be recycled and reformed into cork boards and a different style of wine stopper. The one thing that is beneficial to cork is also its most troubling problem, it's a natural product. This means that if it happens to be a rotted piece of cork, then the wine inside the bottle that it's stopping will also become spoiled. Annual natural cork taint is responsible for nearly 10% of ruined wine. One out of every ten bottles stopped with natural cork runs the risk of being spoiled. Imagine if one out of every ten boxes of your cereal went bad or you had to throw away one out of every ten pork chops you bought. You would start to look for new ways to package your Lucky Charms.

Many attempts were made to reduce this percentage and these alternatives are very effective. The first attempts were similar to beer bottle tops which some Proseccos still use. There are also flexible plastic corks that have the look and feel of natural corks. A variation on the plastic cork is the Zork, which is a trademarked name for a plastic cork with a hard, plastic cap for easy removal. Finally, the one closure that gets a lot of people's panties in a wad is the screw cap. People have this notion that screw caps are for low rent wine. Well, have you ever heard of a bottle of Boone's Farm going bad? You haven't because the folks at Boone's knew that screw caps work very well. If you're planning on drinking the wine that you bought sometime in the next twelve months, then get it with a screw cap. If you're an investor and you're planning on cellaring some expensive Cabernets for the next 10 to 20 years, then your best bet is to risk the possibility of cork taint and buy wine corked with natural corks. The sooner people get over the false sense of posh corks, the quicker they will discover wine that is sure to be good with an alternative closure.

The need for a good closure is to ensure the wine doesn't go bad. Even with a fool proof enclosure, wine can still go bad. There are a few reasons that wine spoils, air and heat being the two main culprits. The first problem is one that I mentioned above, cork taint. If the cork is bad, the wine is bad. Easy as that.

The second is overexposure to air. If you open a bottle and don't drink it all, you only have a couple of days before that wine technically goes bad. It might still taste like wine four days from now, but it doesn't taste nearly as good as it did when you first opened it, and it could cause a stomach ache because it is perishable. If you open it, try to get it all in your belly within three days. This will save your stomach from revolting on you. Fortified wines like port and sherry are the exception to this rule. Their higher alcohol content gives them a far longer shelf life after you open it. Weeks for sure, possibly months.

The third destroyer of wine is heat. If you're going shopping or to the gun range, make the wine store your last stop. If your wine spends twenty minutes in a 100-degree car, it is ruined. Again, wine is a perishable food. You wouldn't leave a tuna salad sandwich sitting in the sun on the seat of your car while you ran in to try on dresses or combat boots. The same applies to wine. It will spoil in the heat.

So how do you know if a wine has gone bad? There are a few telltale signs. Here are three tests you can do to determine if you'll be enjoying a glass of wine or crying as you dump it down the drain.

Test 1:
Sight. If it's a white wine, you can first tell by seeing if the color is off. If it has turned deep, ugly yellow or rotten banana brown, you probably need to turn your bottle upside down in the sink and watch it swirl out of your life. If it is still a relatively normal pale yellow, you are probably in the clear. Red wine can be red whether it's good or bad. Some reds, however, can turn brown and you'll be able to see it when you pour it into the glass. Don't rely solely on color to determine if your wine is good or not. There are so many variations of wine color that you might dump a perfectly good bottle if you don't use tests 2 and 3.

Test 2:
Smell. When you remove the cork or cap, put your schnozz over the opening and take a whiff. Does it smell like all the other wine that you've smelled? Then you're probably good to go. However, if you get a strange odor, you might be feeding the sink. Bad wine can smell like a number of different things. It can have odors of mildew, wet cardboard, dirt, acid, urine, vinegar, or body odor. Nasty, right? If you sniff your wine and it makes you think of your home gym in the basement, you need to throw it out. If it passes the sniffer test, then move on to the final test.

Test 3:
Taste. This one is pretty simple. Once you get it into the glass, or coffee mug, or Viking drinking horn, then all you have to do is sip it. If it has gone bad, it will probably taste like the things I mention in Test 2, dank basement. (Dank Basement. Cool band name. I call it.) If it tastes like all the other wines you've tried, then kick back and enjoy your adult beverage.

How Long Will My Wine Last after I've opened it?

Red Wine – 3 to 5 Days
White Wine – 3 to 7 Days
Full bodied white wines like Chardonnay will last closer to 3 days while lighter wines like Pinot Grigio can last up to 7.
Pink Wine – 4 to 7 Days

Sparkling Wine – 1 to 3 Days, The bubbles could disappear a
as soon as the same day, but the wine will still be good for a
few days.
Bag In A Box Wine – 30 Days
Fortified Wine – 30 Days

All of these are estimates. If you put it in the fridge, it might last a little longer. If you use a vacuum product to suck the air out of the bottle, you can add another couple of days. If you're lucky enough to have one of those dispensers that exchanges nitrogen for the air in the bottle, then you can take your time and enjoy every drop of that wine.

Storing Wine

Ideally, you should get a dual temperature wine refrigerator so you can store reds at one temp and white at another. Realistically, you can just store wine in a darker place like a cabinet, the fridge, or, for larger wine collections, a salt mine. Keeping them in the dark will assure you that the wine isn't being damaged by sunlight. After you've opened it, put it back in a dark place. Leaving it on your kitchen counter is fine as long as it stays out of direct sunlight. Put white wines back in the fridge with the cap or cork on. I didn't do that once and spilled a half bottle of Riesling all over a pizza. It totally ruined my plan for leftovers.

Serving Wine

Temperature

Sparkling Wine – Ice Cold

I think we've all seen a movie where a couple in a restaurant orders Champagne and the waiter sets an ice bucket beside the table with the bottle in it. This is because Champagne is best served ice cold. It's also why you only fill the glass half full. I know a full glass seems like it would be better, but the more time the wine spends in the glass, the warmer it gets. The warmer it gets, the less enjoyable it becomes. So, if you say "Fill 'er up, garçon" to the waiter, they will make fun of you when they go back to the kitchen.

White Wine and Rosé – Fridge Temperature

Even though there are quite a few different types of white wine, the temp you should serve them is pretty much the same. If you store a white wine in the fridge, you're ready to go. Open and enjoy. If it's on a shelf somewhere, give it a couple of hours to cool down before you drink it. A little time in the freezer can get you there quicker, but don't forget that it's in there. It will freeze and explode. From personal experience, it looks cool, but it's hell to clean up.

Light Red – Chilled

Lighter style red wines like Pinot Noir, Gamay, Grenache, and some Italian wines really blossom when they have a little chill to them. The term "Chilled" is kind of a politician word, it could mean a lot of things without committing to an exact answer. And the trick is to find out how chilled you want your wine. There are wines like Beaujolais that I have no problem putting it in the refrigerator for an hour or two. But I like Pinot Noir chilled a little. I might chill it for twenty minutes in the fridge or, if it's from my dark cool wine cabinet, I'll just open it as it is. Different wines, different qualities, different temperatures. I've said it before and I'll say it again, experiment to find your comfort level.

Heavy Reds - Cool

There are a whole lot of people that say you should serve red wines at room temperature. Well, if you're sitting in a room that's 85 degrees, your wine is going to be 85 degrees too. I like to use the term cellar temperature. Imagine how cool a cave is and that's the temp your reds should be. If you have a Cabernet, Merlot, Zinfandel, etc., pop it in the fridge for 15 to 20 minutes to get it a little cooler than it was sitting on your kitchen counter. If it warms back up after you open it, that's okay. It's not going to ruin your experience. It's just that a tad cooler simply makes it more enjoyable. Not cold! Cool.

Fortified Wine – Cool

Much like the Heavy Reds, if you store port and sherry in a cool dark place, you're all set on the right temperature to serve them. There is no harm in chilling them in the fridge, but the flavors will definitely be muted the colder they are.

Glassware

There are over 20 different glasses that are used to serve wine. There are special glasses for port, sherry, Champagne, Burgundy, Bordeaux Rouge, Bordeaux White, and on and on and on. Some of them look very similar to others, but there is a purpose for each one. Bordeaux glasses are larger so you can swirl a wine with higher tannings to aerate it before you drink it. Champagne flutes channel the bubbles to hold the effervescence longer. White wine glasses are smaller so the wine will stay cool as you drink it. All of these aspects make for a better wine experience and there is an enhancement to your wine experience when you drink it from the proper glass. However, if you're like me and you have a limited budget and no extra space for glassware, you can get away with having larger ones for red, smaller ones for white, Champagne flutes if you love sparkling wine or Mimosas. For the average wine drinker that is enjoying a Pinot Noir with their grilled pork chops, the subtle nuances that are offered by a Burgundy glass will probably be missed. Don't feel bad about being an average wine drinker. The important part is that you're a wine drinker and you're enjoying it. So, lift a glass, any glass, and give a toast to yourself for being in AWEC, Average Wine Enjoyer's Club. I'm not just the founder, I'm also a member!

Another thing that some wine drinkers use is a decanter. When a wine gets to a certain age, it begins to develop sediment in the bottle. It's totally natural. It's just tiny bits of stems, grape skins, and seeds that didn't get filtered out. While it is natural, it can be gross if you happen to get a mouthful of grit and squishiness. Enter the decanter. You can delicately pour the wine into the decanter as you watch to make sure there is no sediment getting into the decanter. It helps to shine a flashlight through the bottle so you can see what's moving around in there. If you're like me and you know you're not that talented at the delicate pour, you can filter an older wine through a piece of cheesecloth. It's a bit inelegant, but it gets the job done. For most of us, we're not opening a 42-year-old bottle of Petrus, so decanting to remove sediment isn't necessary. However, decanting a red wine also aerates the wine so the tannins will dissipate making it smoother and tastier. Putting wine in a decanter also makes it easier to pour at dinners and parties. Another plus is it looks fancier than having a bottle on the table. The downside to decanters is some of them are a pain in the ass to clean. But there are bendable brushes to help with that chore.

In the end, what we're all trying to do is have a decent glass of wine and not spend half of our food budget to do it. Luckily for us, wines from all over the world are available at your local wine shop. Find a Chilean Cabernet or a Spanish Rioja and try it. Don't be a snob and balk at the sight of a screw cap. Take it home, serve it with dinner, and discover what our ancestors knew; any meal can be better with the right wine and the right friends. Cheers.

Important Abbreviations and Words on Wine Labels

Italy

IGT – Indication of Geographical Typicality: This is the broadest of the quality designations used in Italy. And by quality, I mean quality based on the government's criteria. IGT wines are good and wide ranging in taste. They're table wines that you'll find in restaurants as their house wine and inexpensive bottles in wine shops. This doesn't necessarily lower the quality, but the government has no way of verifying the quality so they just lump them all into IGT. A lot of them are tasty, cheap, and uncomplicated. However, IGTs are also the highly sought-after wines called Super Tuscans. They fit in this category since they are not made with the exact grapes that are legal to grow in Tuscany to make it a DOC wine. Like everything, sometimes the government's rules don't fit reality.

DOC – Controlled Designation of Origin: These wines are a little more refined than the IGTs. According to the Italian powers that be, these wines must be made from specific grapes from a specific area, like Montepulciano grapes from the Montepulciano area. Each area is a small designated area and has a limit to the number of grapes per acre they can grow, also called harvest yields. They must adhere to aging minimums, barrel usage, and alcohol content. Following these guidelines, an area can be elevated to DOC. This assures the buyer of a higher quality product. You will be able to find a government sticker on each bottle indicating it's been checked.

DOCG – Controlled and Guaranteed Designation of Origin: This is the top tier according to government standards. They must adhere to the same rules as the DOC wines and they must be from an even smaller area than the DOCs. These wines are taste tested by the government licensed Judgment Panel. Nice work if you can get it. If the wine passes their approval, they are given a numbered government "Guarantee Seal" sticker for each cork or cap. This is another indicator to the buyer that the wine is what the label promises.

All of this government involvement is because in the past, people weren't always buying the same level of wine that merchants were selling. Unethical retailers were buying bulk wine and putting a high-end label on it and selling for a premium. Italy didn't want their wine industry to become a joke so they began enforcing regulations. While I'm not always a fan of government overreach, this was a good move on their part. It keeps people honest and keeps us from needlessly paying too much for good wine.

France

VSIG – Vin Sans Indication Geographique: These are also called VT or Vin de Table. Basically, they're wines from no geographical area recognized by the French government. Kind of like a wine that only has "California" on the label. California is a big state. It could be from anywhere. There's nothing wrong with it. It just comes from a vague part of France. Like the IGT wines from Italy, most are tasty and inexpensive.

Vin de Pays – (Spoken just like it looks except don't pronounce the s on the end) These are what some people call Country Wine. They are made in outlying areas like the vast area Languedoc (LONG-doc) and Loire (lo-Wahr). In order to earn this designation, the producers must submit the wine to a committee and follow some simple guidelines for production like specific grapes in a specific area and harvest yields. Once approved, they can label them Vin de Pays.

The more French wines you try, you may discover that you like wine from a particular region. To help you, there are a few subcategories of VdPs that you can watch out for when you're buying. They are Vin de Pays de la Loire, Vin de Pays du Comté Tolosan, Vin de Pays Méditerranée, and Vin de Pays des Comtés Rhodaniens. There are a few new ones that are being disputed so I won't bother with those. Maybe if they're agreed upon, the second edition might have them.

AOC – Appellation d'Origine Controlee: These are the top-notch designated wines in France. The French government holds the wineries in this category to a very high standard of quality. They are restricted to the same rules as the Vin de Pays and a few extra ones, but to a much stricter degree. It may seem like a bit of overkill, but France is insanely serious about their wine industry. And the proof is in every bottle of French wine you buy. Some of the AOC regions that you may see out there are Bordeaux, Chablis (Not the cheap shit in a gallon jug), Champagne, and Côtes du Rhône. There are well over a hundred different AOC regions and they are all held to the highest standards that France has to offer. And who wins because of their work? Yep. We do. Vive le France!

Spain

Crianza – This is a red wine that was aged in oak barrels for at least one year.

Reserva – Wines that have been aged at least two years and at least one year in oak barrels can be upgraded to a Reserva.

Gran Reserva – If you're thinking that these are aged even longer, you'd be right. They are aged at least five years with two years in oak barrels. I've seen some Gran Reserva wines that were aged 10 years. They were magnificent.

DO – Denominacion de Origen: Similar to Italy's DOC, Spain's DO has guidelines that must be followed to ensure quality; harvest yields, type of grapes used, barrel usage. There are quite a few DOs in Spain and you can buy confidently because they're all being evaluated for quality assurance.

DOCa – Denominacion de Origen Calificada: Like France's AOC, the DOCa is the top tier in Spain. It's such a restricted qualification that there are only two areas that have earned the DOCa designation. If you see Rioja or Priorat on the label, you're getting the best of Spain.

Germany

Qualitatswein (Kwal-eh-TAHTS-vine) – These are the table wines of Germany. Like VTs in France and IGTs in Italy, they are house wines in restaurants and most people's everyday wines. Cheap and tasty.

Kabinett (KAB-ih-net) – This lightest style of Riesling is also the least sweet. They are often dry or have a tinge of sweetness with all the flavors of Riesling.

Spätlese (SHPAT-leh-seh) — The word means Late Harvest and they are sweeter than Kabinett. Although if the word *Trocken* is also on the label, it's a dry Riesling with a higher alcohol content. Confused yet? Oh, I'm just getting warmed up.

Auslese (OWS-leh-seh) — This word means Select Harvest. One step sweeter than Spätlese, these are grapes that are hand selected after Noble Rot has set in. If you spot Trocken on this label, you know it's higher in alcohol.

Beerenauslese (BEER-uhn-ows-leh-seh) — The translation is Berry Selected Harvest and they're a step higher on the sugar levels. The grapes have Noble Rot like the Auslese, but they're so covered in fungus that they become raisins on the vines. Then they're harvested and turned into dessert wine. Nearly all are sold in half bottles and get pretty pricy.

Eiswein (ICE-vine) These dessert wines are about the same sweetness level as Beerenauslese wines. The difference is they are harvested when the grapes have frozen on the vines. The water inside the grape freezes and the nectar is pressed out. These are also pretty expensive. These wines are not only from Germany, Canada makes some fantastic versions too.

Trockenbeerenauslese (TROKE-uhn-beer-uhn-ows-leh-seh). The sweetest of the sweet wines. The grapes for this wine have taken on Noble Rot and have completely turned to raisins on the vine, hence the Trocken (German for Dry) part of the word. Without grape juice to dilute the nectar, the liquid that gets pressed out of the raisin makes a ridiculously sweet wine with all the luxurious qualities you would expect from a bottle that might equal a car payment.

That wraps up the German labels. Practice saying the words. Get them down pat and go ask for them at your favorite store. Chances are pretty good that you will pronounce them better than the clerk ringing them up.

The Rest Is Bullshit

There are hundreds of other definitions and explanations that could be added to this section, but that would be needlessly excessive. I brought you the important things to know. If you want to learn further, there are a ton of cerebral works out there for your reading pleasure. As for me and my book, that's quite enough. Well, except for the ending thoughts.

Congratulations! You are now a qualified professional. Go shop with confidence. Also, feel free to use the Crum Rinse as needed. Result may vary.

Okay, Let's Wrap It Up

In the early part of 2020, I played the role of The Librarian in a production of "Underneath the Lintel" by playwright Glen Berger. It's a great script for a one-man show. It was late December of 2019 and I was slated to perform it in late April. Plenty of time to get ready for a show that would be only me speaking for an hour and a half. As life so often throws curveballs, another play that was supposed to be produced starting February 1st was cancelled with no alternative to put in its place.

So, I was asked if I could move my show up a couple of months. With a panic burning in my brain, I said yes. I read through the play hundreds of times, recorded me saying the words so I could listen to it when I wasn't able to read it, memorized it, collected props and set pieces, and worked diligently on the delivery of the words. I was able to put a pretty good show together in a shorter amount of time. I made it through eight performances. Some shows were full and some weren't. That time of year in Oklahoma, the weather can be nasty and unpredictable. Doing that show proved that I could achieve things I didn't think I was capable of. That confidence led me to finally finish this book.

After that show's run was over, Covid-19 took over the country and the theatres were shut down. If I hadn't had the show moved up, I probably wouldn't have been able to do it at all. It sounds trite, but everything happens for a reason.

It's the same with this book. I was working at a major bookstore chain when I decided to go to bartending school. I graduated and looked for work slinging drinks. I walked into a French restaurant and told the guy I was there about the bartender job. He told me to start work that night. One of the other owners walked in that night and wondered who the hell I was. He didn't want to hire me, just interview me. He thought I might as well stay since I was already there.

From there I went to work at a premier wine shop, then a distributor, then a better distributor. I quit all that and moved closer to my parents so they could watch our daughter grow up. When I got to the little town, I went to work for a small vineyard and horse ranch. Then I went to work for a bigger vineyard. Then I found a little liquor store within walking distance of my house. I went there and gave them my resume. He didn't want to hire me because he thought I was way overqualified for his "chicken shit little store". I assured him that I just wanted a part time job while I worked on other things. He enthusiastically hired me and became one of the best friends I've had to date.

One thing led to another which led to another which led to another. Everything happens for a reason. All of that "led to another" resulted in this book and my website www.TheNoBSWinePage. com (Shameless Plug). I hope my book has been a good read for you. I hope you now know some things you didn't know before. I hope it encourages you to go out and find your favorite new wine. I also hope it encourages you to keep doing what you're doing to get to where you want to be. Cheers!

I am thankful for every step I have taken to get me to the next sentence. The End.

The
Recognitions

Lots of books have pages where the author lists a bunch of people that contributed help along the way. I have a list too, but for most people, I either can't remember their names or I never knew their names. I remember little encounters. I remember faces. Names? Not so much. To all the people who have ever given me a bit of advice, or a factoid, or a joke, or a story that meant something to me, I appreciate you. Whether you knew it at the time or not, you've helped me get to this point. Thanks.

For the people whose names I do remember, this is your section. To my wife, Flora, you are my inspiration, my support system, my cheerleader, my second editor, and my best friend. I love you forever. Thank you for still wanting to kiss me. To my daughter Audry, thank you for being a loving kid and an inspiration for what is possible in the world. My mom and dad, Jim and Twila. Pretty much everything in my life happened because I had the love and support of great parents. I appreciate you immensely. My brother Jeff and his wife Suzanne will always be on my favorite people list. Thank you for being my family and always supporting whatever hairbrained activity I've found myself a part of. The crew at Grand Spirits; Henri (I can still hear his voice in my head), Linda, Kara, Clark, and all those that have come and gone from there, I appreciate that you've included me as one of your family. To Travis, my first editor, I appreciate the help and the gentle question of "How's the book coming?" You knew it was important to me. The folks at Joe Saglimbeni's in San Antonio circa 1999; Joe, Robert, Mike, Al, Curtis, and Sue. An endless supply of information came from all of us selling wine, drinking wine, and telling stories. I will forever use the "Crum rinse" during wine tastings. All the sales staff at Glazer's in San Antonio in the early 2000's. I learned so much from all of you. I can't imagine my time on this planet without that experience. Lastly, the place where I began my Wine Life journey, L'Etoile. Armand, Thierry, and Frederick offered me the opportunity to try amazing wines and showed me which wines were elite, which ones tasted good, what were average wines, and if a wine should be labeled "C'est d'la merde". Merci, gentlemen. Lastly, to all the people that I have been in theatre with at Playmakers. I know it has nothing to do with wine, but the love and inspiration, persistence and gumption that we've lived through have shaped who I am today. I can never thank you enough.

To everyone on my list:

"I love thee with a love that shall not die, till the sun grows cold and the stars grow old."

—Bill Shakespeare